TERRY MARSH

ON FOOT IN THE LAKE DISTRICT

Northern
& Western Fells

DAVID & CHARLES

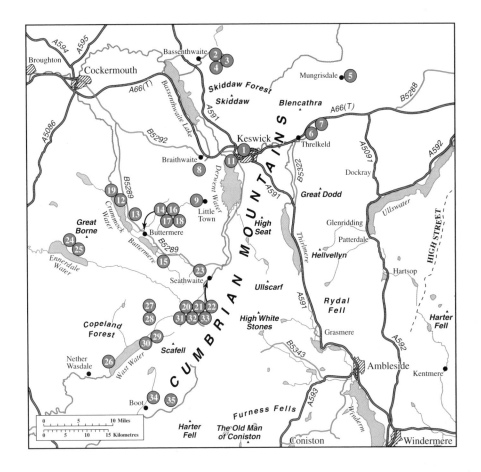

All photographs and maps are by the author

This book has been compiled in accordance with the *Guidelines for the Writers of Path Guides* produced by the Outdoor Writers' Guild. Every effort has been made to ensure that the information it contains about pathways is accurate, but changes do occur and the author would welcome notification of any such changes, through the publisher.

A DAVID & CHARLES BOOK

First published in the UK in 1997

Typeset by ABM Typographics Ltd, Hull
Printed in Italy by Milanostampa SpA
for David & Charles
Brunel House Newton Abbot Devon

Front cover photo: Wasdale
Back cover photo: Mellbreak and Crummock Water from Ling Comb
Page 1: Ascending beside Taylorgill Force

CONTENTS

INTRODUCTION

It is hard to imagine there could be anyone left in Britain who does not know of the renowned beauties of Lakeland, yet each year I meet people visiting the region for the first time. While tramping contentedly across Esk Hause late one idyllic afternoon under the guise of working on this book, I met a heavily laden couple convinced that the shapely peak of Ill Crag was their intended objective, Scafell Pike. I disillusioned them, but they told me that they had read, somewhere, that amid all the Pike's rocks there is, near the summit, a small oasis of green grass and on it they planned to pitch their tent in order to watch the sun rise. Their intention could not be faulted, but their act of faith was beyond my comprehension; there is indeed a patch of grass that will take a tent, but not much more, but to travel from Kent, as they had, in search of it, merely served to remind me how charismatic the Lake District can be and how taken for granted, by we frequent visitors, who should know better. After all, I can still remember a school geography lesson almost forty years ago when the master put up a colour slide of Napes Needle and asked if anyone knew where or what it was. All but one in my class seemed to know the answer and another ten years would pass before I

did, but in those soft grey dusky days of youth, engrossed in the hardships and limitations of a coal mining community in Lancashire, I had never heard of the Lake District, let alone Napes Needle.

All that, thankfully, was to change, and it came to be a change for which I shall be eternally grateful.

When it came, my first visit to the Lake District took me on part of the Coledale Horseshoe, drawn there no doubt by the fascinating skyline of Causey Pike and the seemingly endless flow of mountains beyond. Armoured by the ignorance of youthfulness, I had soon stumbled into most of the corners of Lakeland, oblivious to the potential dangers and only aware of the new sensations of wonder that were assaulting my senses. Many years later I read Thomas Gray and his description of the heart of the district, a 'turbulent chaos of mountain behind mountain, rolled in confusion'. Almost two hundred years later, the Lake District was having the same impact on me and the memory of this helped me to put in perspective the ambitions and keenness of my Esk Hause soulmates.

This process of revelation is a key element in the character of the Lakes. Before long

everyone knows the basic geography, the different mountain groups, the names of the various lakes and many of the tarns, the highest summits and so on. But then comes a much closer acquaintance, as if the spirit of the district has decided to reveal some of its secrets, just a few at a time, enough to whet the appetite for more. One day, as happened to me, you are driving down Borrowdale and suddenly the great lake of Derwent Water, normally dotted with sailing boats, is for once mirror still, reflecting the undulations of Cat Bells and Maiden Moor so faithfully, with breath-holding perfection, that when you look at the resulting picture you can invert it, and not know for sure which way is correct. Or you find yourself so peacefully wrapped in the embrace of some fellside rock that neither the feeding rabbits at your feet nor the golden eagle sliding by overhead see you there and go about their business unheeding of your presence.

It is not by chance that the Lake poets found so much to say about the Lakes, nor happenstance that turns the modern visitor westwards from the M6 motorway; it is a

Right: The head of Wasdale

The green fields of Wasdale from Yewbarrow

I began this book and its companion volume, almost ten years had gone by since I completed work on my first Lakeland books; ten years in which I rarely returned to the Lakes, ten years when I was always somewhere else – the Alps, the Pyrenees, the Yorkshire Dales, southern Scotland, the Isle of Skye, the Pennines and more. No hardship, I confess, in being there, but what a delight to return, to travel familiar trails, to wander peacefully with my dogs through fondly remembered remote valleys, to remember the many days spent among these magnificent fells with friends and chance acquaintances, to recall the sights and sounds, the mysteries and magic of earlier times.

In presenting this collection of walks, I have been at pains to put forward routes that give a true flavour of everything that is good, and to illustrate them, in all the seasons, to serve as an inspiration both to those who are venturing for the first time as walkers to Lakeland, and those who know and love the unique *mélange* of lakes, rivers, fells, valleys, towns and villages with an abiding affection. The walks have been chosen for their intrinsic quality, accessibility and their character; in a very finite work, there are countless permutations that had to be omitted. That should dissuade no one from using these walks as a basic introduction, and from there launching into what will prove to be many years of exploration, enjoyment and reward on foot in the Lake District.

charisma that is unique, a penetrating beauty, a subtle juxtaposition of ingredients and a social history as fascinating as any.

Compared with mountain ranges elsewhere, the Lakeland summits are modest. Yet they can be as severe and extreme as any.

Those visited by walks in this volume include the very highest and roughest, being spectacular and hugely rewarding on days of crystal clarity, but daunting, grim and dangerous when lashed by the torment of an evil winter.

It is one of the burdens of a professional outdoor writer that work often leads you away from the places you enjoy most. When

EXPLANATORY NOTES

The Walks

With over five hundred fell tops in the Lake District, it follows that there are an enormous number of ways of reaching their summits and of devising routes between them. The thirty-five walks contained in this volume can do no more than hint at the possibilities, but it is a hint with a distinct flavour, one intended to encourage the reader to begin an exploration of this remarkable and popular region.

Most of the walks are circular, while some are linear in the sense that it is necessary to return by the outward route. Almost all follow clear paths, but where this is not so, a note to that effect is given in the text, usually advising that the walk is not to be attempted in poor visibility.

None of the walks presents technical difficulties in good conditions in summer. Most are walks, not climbs, though a few – Napes on Great Gable and Sharp Edge on Blencathra, for example – need the ability to scramble. The majority of the walks can also be completed in good winter conditions, but when snow and ice prevail an ice axe is essential and crampons may be needed from time to time.

Maps

The Ordnance Survey Outdoor Leisure maps, to a scale of 1:25 000 (2in to 1 mile–4cm to 1km), Sheets 4 (The English Lakes North Western Area) and 6 (The English Lakes South Western Area), cover all but the most northerly of the walks and provide excellent detail.

The Ordnance Survey Landranger Series, Sheets 89 (West Cumbria) and 90 (Penrith, Keswick and Ambleside), at a scale of 1:50 000 (1¼in to 1 mile–2cm to 1km) cover the walks fully.

Harveys produce three maps – Northern Lakeland, North West Lakeland and Western Lakeland – which cover the entire area dealt with in this volume. These maps, intended specifically for walkers, are in two forms: one, the conventional Walker's series, at a scale of 1:40 000 (2.5cm to 1km), the other, the Superwalker series, to a scale of 1:25 000. Both series are produced on waterproof material, show different land usage and are accompanied by visitor guides.

Distances

The stated distances are for the *complete* walk, ie including the return distance on linear walks. They are given in both metric and non-metric and have been rounded up or down.

Height Gain

This reflects the total ascent for the walk as described, not just the height gain from the start to the top of a fell.

Walking Times

These represent a realistic allowance for a walker of average fitness, but it must be stressed **they make no allowance for stops**, other than brief halts to take pictures.

Sections and Section Names

These are quite arbitrary and should not be taken too seriously; they are simply creatures of convenience.

Access

It is unlikely you will be challenged on any of these walks if you stick to the routes described. But the Lake District is a working environment, one that needs to be sensitively treated by visitors. Any mention of a path **does not imply that a right of way exists**. If you are asked not to follow a particular route, please comply, as there is invariably a good reason for doing so.

If you take your dog with you, please ensure it is held on a leash at all times. Do not allow your dog to run about unrestrained.

1

THE NORTHERN FELLS

Concealed from view by the combined mass of Skiddaw and Blencathra, the windswept moors that formed part of the medieval Forest of Skiddaw, where the barons of Greystoke 'suffered the porklins to run wild in the woods', are today an infrequently visited arena, grazing for sheep and passed through with almost indecent haste by Lakeland's only creditable long-distance walk, the Cumbria Way. Only the fleeting glimpse of conical Great Calva through the defile of Glenderaterra Beck suggests there may be something hidden behind the bold façade of mountain might with which visitors to northern Lakeland bound for Keswick and beyond are familiar; there is! – an unmistakably wild and intriguing place, with no equal in the Lake District. Possessing wide, smooth-flanked valleys, broad grass- and heather-cloaked uplands and sprawling boggy flats more akin to the not-so-distant Pennines than to the craggy countenance of Lakeland to which we are more accustomed, this inner sanctum is a place of special favour with connoisseurs of Lakeland walking.

Here, Back o' Skidda', among that 'noiseless noise which lives in the summer air', those in

On the northern slopes of Skiddaw

search of solitude will find a corner of Heaven, a haven from the drama of the main stage upon which the mountains, lakes, towns and villages of Cumbria play out their role as hosts to the nation's tourists and walking fraternity. With no view of the heart of Lakeland to suggest otherwise, among these unassuming fells you could be a million miles from the brouhaha of Windermere, Ambleside and Keswick, emerging at the end of the day into the 'real' world, refreshed by a brief hibernation.

In the middle of this moorland wilderness, surrounded by the only stand of trees of note, a windbreak of larch, is a row of former cottages, Skiddaw House, all that remains now, that and a few circular sheepfolds, to tell of the hardships and hardiness of the Lakeland shepherds who used this isolated retreat as their base until the last shepherd retired in 1969. Formerly a shooting lodge, a bothy, and a school outdoor centre, Skiddaw House is now used as a youth hostel and must shine like the most brilliant beacon to Cumbrian wayfarers caught by a sudden change in the weather, or overtaken by nightfall.

These hidden fells were once the hunting ground of John Peel, who was born in Caldbeck in 1776, and celebrated in song in his own lifetime by his friend John Woodcock

Graves. 'D'ye ken John Peel' set to a Scottish air must be Cumbria's most famous folk song.

The rocks that make up the whole of the Northern Fells are the oldest in the Lake District, known as Skiddaw Slates, and date from Ordovician times, up to 500 million years ago. These are flaky, fine-grained, darkly coloured sedimentary rocks formed on the bed of some ancient sea when life on earth had scarcely begun, and only then as minute creatures, trilobites and graptolites, today detectable by a knowledgeable eye as white streaks in the darkness of the rock. Slates they may be, but they are a far cry from the beautiful blue-green slates quarried elsewhere in the Lake District for roofing and building.

Much of this fine detail, however, will pass unnoticed beneath the feet of most walkers who will have their eyes turned to the heights of the main summits: Skiddaw, the highest, and Blencathra, arguably the most rewarding. Not surprisingly, since their gaze cannot be avoided, frowning as they do upon the little ways of Man, Skiddaw and Blencathra caught the attention of the early visitors to Lakeland, Thomas Gray, Coleridge, Southey and the Wordsworths.

Coleridge lived at Greta Hall in nearby Keswick from 1800-1803, from where he

wrote to his brother-in-law and immediate successor at Greta Hall, Robert Southey, saying, 'Behind us the massy Skiddaw, smooth, green, high, with two chasms and a tent-like ridge in the larger. A fairer scene you have not seen in all your wanderings'. Southey stayed at Greta Hall for forty years, so it is easy to understand how he came to mention 'My neighbour Skiddaw', for nowhere in Britain does a mountain so dominate a town as Skiddaw does Keswick. Before the thirteenth century, however, Skiddaw would have gazed only upon the muddy flats of the Vale of Keswick, for in spite of its apparent foreverness, Keswick is comparatively new.

The first mention of its name appears in the mid-thirteenth century when the monks of Furness Abbey were granted permission to construct a mill dam on the Greta at 'Kesewic' – a place name that signifies 'cheese village', or a dairy farming settlement. Though this existed from the late seventh century there is little supporting evidence that there was a town here at the time, or even a village, other than that which had accrued around the ancient church site at Crosthwaite. But Keswick grew quickly and in 1276 was granted the right to a hold a weekly market 'procur'd for it of Edward the first by Thomas of Derwentwater, Lord of the place'. By the end of the thirteenth century

Left: Morning mist over Lonscale Fell from Skiddaw House
Right: Blencathra from the summit of Skiddaw

there were some thirty tenants of the manor of Castlerigg 'who hold in burgage in a place called Kewswik'.

'Skiddaw is about eleven hundred yards perpendicular from the Broadwater (i.e. Bassenthwaite Lake). It rises with two heads, like unto Parnassus; and with a kind of emulation beholds Scruffel (Criffel) hill before it in Annandale in Scotland. By these two mountains, according as the misty clouds rise or fall, the people dwelling thereabouts make their prognostication of the change of the weather.'

Such was the opinion of Joseph Nicolson and Richard Burn writing in 1777, capturing the essence of country weather lore.

But among the Northern Fells Skiddaw is not alone in providing excellent walking; neighbouring Blencathra could claim to be by far a much finer mountain. Its five main southern ridges, shaped by glacial action into splendid arêtes, offer walkers a variety of ascents and descents that must rank highly on any serious walker's list of favourite routes.

On Blencathra – known also as Linthwaite Pike, Threlkeld Fell, Blencrater, Blenkarthur and Saddleback – you could spend a week or more exploring its ridges and secretive corries, and ascending to its neat summit each day by a different route.

Such diversity of walking opportunity is characteristic of the Northern Fells, making them worthy participants in the role the Lake District plays for those who enjoy their experiences at a genteel pace, on foot.

SKIDDAW FROM KESWICK

Skiddaw and Little Man

The graceful lines of Skiddaw, towering high above the ancient market town of Keswick to which it provides a most beautiful backdrop, are a challenge no red-blooded walker can ignore for long. Formed from the oldest rocks in Lakeland, Skiddaw and its acolytes are irresistible, made doubly so by the apparent ease of ascent its simple, graceful lines suggest.

Many walkers seek to minimise the haul to this sixth highest summit in the Lake District by starting from the top of Gale Road, reached via Underscar, and then simply hasten back the way they came. Yet the full climb from Keswick town centre adds little demand for energy. By contrast, to complete the full circuit described here, a good measure of fitness is called for, set against which the reward – a fine, and often solitary, excursion into the heart of the region known as 'Back o' Skidda' – more than justifies the effort.

Begin from Keswick by locating and crossing the River Greta to enter Fitz Park. There, cross diagonally left to a narrow walkway leading on to a quiet back road near the abutments of an old railway bridge. Go right here and walk up to Spooney Green Lane, which will lead you across the A66 and up into the wooded pleasantness of lower Latrigg. By following the main trail you eventually arrive at the top of Gale Road **(1)**, feeling infinitely superior to those who have driven up.

Go right, to a gate and stile, and immediately left along a narrow pathway that leads to a monument perched on a small mound **(2)**. The monument is to three shepherds of the Hawell family, noted for their skill in breeding the ubiquitous Herdwick sheep of Lakeland. The inscription reads:

> *Great Shepherd of Thy heavenly flock*
> *These men have left our hill*
> *Their feet were on the living rock*
> *Oh guide and bless them still.*

Beyond the monument the long slope of Jenkin Hill looms, an obvious, well-trodden trail leading unendingly upwards, or so it seems. By this route, the first tourists would ascend Skiddaw, an undertaking described by one contemporary author as 'easy, even for ladies, who have only to sit their ponies to find themselves at the top, after a ride of six miles'. Another writer, however, finds the ascent 'very fatiguing' and recommends taking a guide and 'sandwiches and brandy, to recruit their strength previous to the descent'.

Yet the apparent toil of Jenkin Hill succumbs to a steady, gentle plod, leading to a more relaxed gradient as the twin-topped summit of Little Man comes into view. Good

progress can be made now; as you reach a gate **(3)** and stile at a fenceline, the option of climbing left to take in Little Man itself, its ridge line then being followed to rejoin the fence at another gate. This addition puts another 125m (410ft) on the ascent, without significantly increasing the distance walked.

If you elect to bypass Little Man, continue on a broad track, with fine views across the heartlands of the Skiddaw and Blencathra domain, until, on the approach to a gate through the returning fenceline, the going underfoot noticeably changes, becoming much more stony. A clear trod leads across the rocky summit ridge, first to reach the south summit with the main summit still some distance away. A short down and up quickly brings you to the double shelter, trig and orientation table (commemorating the Queen's Silver Jubilee) that adorn the highest point **(4)**.

Walkers returning directly to Keswick need only retrace their steps, a fine prospect, heading first for the long line of the Dodds and the Helvellyn massif, and then towards the great expanse of Derwent Water.

From the summit press on northwards, keeping in mind, against a decline in visibility, that to your right (east) runs the fenceline encountered earlier, and that this will ultimately lead you safely down to the supply road to Skiddaw House. On a clear day you can simply follow a well-trodden path down Skiddaw's northern ridge to the wide bulge of Broad End. Eventually, the path peters out, so

The Hawell Monument

now is the time to step across to that fence, beside which a narrow trod runs faithfully on. As the fenceline turns acutely, continue with it, descending steeply, facing Little and Great Calva and passing close by the dark slopes of

Start/Finish Keswick town centre, GR 267234.
The walk may be shortened by 5km (3 miles) by
starting at the top of Gale Road, GR 281253
Distance To Skiddaw summit and direct return
14km (8¾ miles). Full circuit 20km (12½ miles)
Height gain Skiddaw summit 850m (2788ft).
Full circuit 945m (3100ft)
Walking time Skiddaw summit
and return 3½-4 hours. Allow 6
hours, for full circuit
Type of walk A high mountain
walk with little shelter from bad
weather; capable of being followed
throughout in poor visibility

The Route in Brief

Start Leave Keswick through Fitz
Park, to reach Spooney Green Lane,
and ascend to the top of Gale Road.
1 Follow narrow path to Hawell
monument.
2 Ascend Jenkin Hill to gate below
Little Man.
3 Continue to summit of Skiddaw
and return (Optional return.)
4 Continue northwards to meet and
follow fenceline down to Whitewater
Dash.
5 Turn R along supply road to
Skiddaw House.
6 From Skiddaw House follow
obvious trail to and below Lonscale
Fell to reach monument again, and
retrace steps from there.

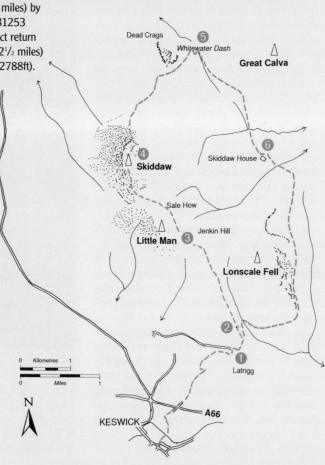

Dead Crags before finally dropping to reach
the road to Skiddaw House close by the charming falls of Whitewater Dash **(5)**, where Dash
Beck plunges attractively across a rock sill.

Nowhere complicated on this walk, the
route finding now becomes even easier as you
follow the long road to Skiddaw House, devi-
ating not at all, save to explore the watery in-
trusions of Dead Beck and the River Caldew.

Skiddaw House **(6)**, formerly a row of cottages, and surrounded by the only trees in what
is known as Skiddaw Forest, was once the
home of shepherds, but now, after a varied history of neglect and usage, sees service as a
youth hostel.

Pass round Skiddaw House to the left, following its wall and then a boggy path, descending gently to cross Salehow Beck by a footbridge. Beyond a gate the path rises to meet a
dilapidated wall. Keep right when the ruins of
sheepfolds and old buildings are encountered.

The onward route now rises ahead of you,
crossing the dramatic slopes of Lonscale Fell,
high above Glenderaterra Beck, with imposing
views of Blease Fell and the other summits of
Blencathra. Eventually, the path rounds
Lonscale Fell, passes through a gate and drops
easily to one of Lakeland's most charming
nooks, as you cross Whit Beck. Only a short
uphill section, the last, is needed to take you
back to the outward route, not far from the
Hawell monument, and from here you simply
retrace your steps to the top of Gale Road and
then down to Keswick.

SKIDDAW AND LONGSIDE EDGE

In spite of a demanding final pull to the south summit, this variant way up Skiddaw is far superior to the 'tourist route' from Keswick by way of Jenkin Hill in every respect except the convenience of its start. But even that proves to be the key to the secrets of Southerndale, neglected by most walkers, and the splendid ridge of Longside Edge, with its outstanding views of Bassenthwaite Lake and the North Western Fells. Walkers who have thus far neglected Longside Edge, need urgently to revise their priorities, the whole ridge, from Ullock Pike to Carl Side, being one of the finest in Lakeland and a sufficient objective in itself.

Begin from a small lay-by along the back road to Orthwaite and Caldbeck, just off the A591. The road is busier than might be expected and a botanical paradise in spring when the hedgerows and verges are bright with wild flowers. A short distance from the lay-by, a gate and nearby stile give access to a large, open pasture. Follow the obvious path until you can leave it, right, to pursue a grassy path along a line of hawthorns. Beyond the hawthorns the path bends left and runs up to a gate and across the ensuing enclosure to another gate before reaching a broad expanse of close-cropped turf, with the grey bulk of Skiddaw looming ahead.

Move half right across the grassy stretch to reach a prominent track and follow this, right, through a gate at the intake wall. Once through the gate the loveliness of hidden Southerndale (1) opens before you, a sweet green dale, rising smooth-flanked to the scree slopes of Skiddaw and Randel Crag on the left, and the conical lure of Ullock Pike and Longside Edge beyond.

Continue into Southerndale and, shortly, ignore a track descending left across Southerndale Beck. Instead, press on a short distance further until you can move right over a series of hillocks called The Edge, near the start of which a group of low standing stones, naturally formed in spite of the suggestion of man's handiwork, will excite a moment's curiosity. They are known as Watches, though with no extant evidence as to why.

With inspired planning, the path ascending Ullock Pike (2) switches from side to side as each new hillock is traversed, giving excellent

Across Southerndale to Longside Edge

Ullock Pike and Longside Edge

views in both directions, before sweeping through heathery braes to the shapely summit.

Now the majesty of Longside Edge reaches out before you, an open and irresistible invitation that extends along this fine ridge with no opportunity for navigational error. The summit of Long Side lies a couple of strides off the path, marked by a small cairn.

From Long Side the ongoing path aims for Skiddaw rather than Carl Side. In good weather this is not a problem, but any lessening of visibility could cause uncertainty. For the avoidance of doubt, stay on the main path to the col beyond Carl Side – it lies at the head of Southerndale and Slades Beck and houses a small pond, Carlside Tarn. From the tarn you can turn abruptly right to gain a path rising to the large cairn on Carl Side. On a clear day a direct approach to Carl Side is perfectly feasible, followed by an easy descent to the tarn.

The view from Carl Side (3) is limited by the bulk of Skiddaw and Little Man, but southwards the afforested slopes of Borrowdale that rise beyond Derwent Water more than compensate and are often sufficient excuse to forego the ensuing assault on Skiddaw. In the event of a turn in the weather, the quickest way back is into Southerndale, where a green path, improving as it descends, leads back to Southerndale Beck bridge.

The continuation to Skiddaw rises northeastwards, a toilsome pull up long scree slopes to the south summit (4) where the main track to Skiddaw appears. Here, turn left, northwards and cross the Middle Top before finally reaching the orientation table and shelter-cairn on High Man.

A return by the same route is a splendid prospect once Carlside Tarn is regained, but my preferred route continues northwards, descending on a distinct path to the broad, grassy North Col, where the path finally expires. As it does, move left, across the col and on to the grassy upper shoulder of Broad End (5). A short way on another path appears and leads down towards Broad End, bringing into view a low path, sweeping backwards into the head of Barkbethdale. As a way down this

is superb, and ends close by the intake wall (6) of Barkbeth Farm. When it does, go left, following the wall down to Southerndale Beck bridge, beyond which a path rises to meet the track used on the outward section of the walk, from where you simply retrace your steps to the Orthwaite road.

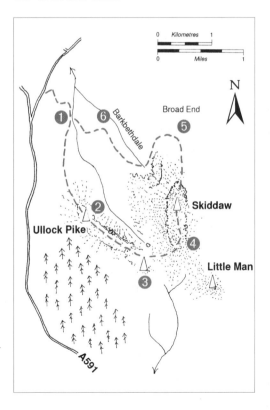

FACT FILE

Start/Finish Lay-by, along the Orthwaite road GR 235295
Distance 11km (7 miles)
Height gain 855m (2805ft)
Walking time 5-6 hours
Type of walk Exhilarating ridge and high mountain walking; some scree. Little protection against bad weather

The Route in Brief
Start From the lay-by, locate gate/stile and follow pathways across fields to reach track at entrance to Southerndale.
1 Go along track through gate/stile and branch R on to The Edge, ascending to Ullock Pike.
2 Continue along ridge to Long Side, Carl Side col and Carl Side.
3 Ascend scree slopes to Skiddaw south summit.
4 Go N to reach main summit, and then descend, still northwards to North Col, there moving L on to upper shoulder of Broad End.
5 Locate path doubling back and down into Barkbethdale, and follow this round dale to intake wall.
6 Go L, above wall, to cross Southerndale Beck, and climb to meet outward route.

SKIDDAW, LONSCALE FELL AND THE DASH FALLS

This uncompromising circuit of Skiddaw leads the walker into parts of the Northern Fells where sheep far outnumber the walkers, and the walkers you do find have a satisfied expression on their faces. For this is a tour of the Skiddaw massif that is without equal, a walk that stands alongside the best in Lakeland.

The key to the walk is a small lay-by along the minor road to Orthwaite, just off the A591. From the lay-by, a few strides up the road bring you to a gate/stile by means of which you access a large field. Follow the obvious path across a stream until, at a waymark, you can leave it, right, to walk beside a diminishing line of hawthorns. A grassy path bends sharply left and leads to another gate, across a second field to a gate, beyond which you stride over a close-cropped sward of sheep pasture, dotted with occasional low gorse bushes.

Bearing right, you soon encounter a broad path **(1)** followed through a gate/stile until you can branch left, and down, to cross Southerndale Beck. Here is Lakeland at its best, a place of simple beauty that will make your heart ache – a place of graceful lines, towering, seemingly unassailable summits and a silence, save for the bleating of lambs and the throaty cronk of a raven overhead.

Descend to cross Southerndale Beck, beyond which a broad, grassy ridge punctuated by small outcrops of slaty rock rises in a succession of bumps to Randel Crag, a fine summit seen from this angle, but in reality little more than a minor wrinkle on Skiddaw's northern face. The objective is to cross this ridge, preferably as low down as possible, following the course of a wall on the left, reached through bracken and heather by an uncertain pathway.

Over the base of the ridge you enter a companion to Southerndale, no less exquisite; this is Barkbethdale **(2)**, beyond which the great nose of Broad End presents a daunting picture. But help is at hand in the form of an old sledgate, branching right, above Barkbethdale Beck, boggy at first, but improving as the head of the dale is reached. Here the path changes direction, heading northwards to pursue a rising trod on to the edge of Broad End, but from this bend the valiant may be tempted by a direct line, one that engages a full frontal assault on slopes of interminable scree and rocks, to the North Col. Only the very fit and experienced go this way.

The rest of us must follow a more pedestrian route on to Broad End **(3)**, where, at a shallow col, a path branches right, less steeply than it seems, on to Broad End and so to the North Col, where a prominent path hastens on to Skiddaw's north top and then the summit **(4)**.

Here the top of the mountain, known as High Man, is a place of rocky carnage, of undulating, and in mist confusing, multiple summits, all of it above 915m (3000ft), and with no defence against the weather save that pitiably offered by tired and ineffective shelters; which is fine – the last place we want a café is on top of Skiddaw!

The ridge southwards offers a fine, rocky promenade along which you will encounter the hordes that have escalated from Keswick. The way is obvious, trodden well into the rocks underfoot, and leads to a gate in a fence **(5)**. Here a broad trail branches left, but leave this and use the fenceline to lead you to the summit of Little Man **(6)**, a misnomer if ever there was one for Little Man is an outstanding summit, with a far better view than that you will gain from its higher sibling.

Using the fenceline as a guide, continue down to rejoin the main path from Keswick near the top of Jenkin Hill, at a gate. Cross to the left, north, side of the fence, leave the main trail behind and follow the fence out towards Lonscale Fell (7) on a grassy trod. In due course a dilapidated wall accompanies the fence, beyond which the path leads to a meeting of fences and a gate with a second gate nearby. Go through the first gate, and follow the fence until you can cross it by a step stile. The fence soon swings away to the right, but here continue ahead to the top of Lonscale Fell, marked by a small cairn, and continue to the lower east top, from which the view of the Glenderaterra Beck far below and the swelling mass of Blease Fell and Blencathra is stunning.

Now you must either retrace your steps towards the gates, without crossing the fence, and from there follow a branching fenceline descending north and north-east, or head directly for the fence from the east top, by locating an initially indistinct pathway that rims above a small corrie. Gradually this peters out, but with the fence in sight, bear right and descend steeply on grassy slopes where care is needed, to gain the undulating ridge of Burnt Horse, across and beyond which a good path leads down beside a wall to meet the Cumbria Way not far from Skiddaw House.

Go left on reaching the valley track, heading

Lonscale Fell

for Skiddaw House (8), passed on its right, beyond which a splendid route whizzes out across the gathering grounds of the River Caldew, crossed by a ford and bridge not far north of Skiddaw House. The trail climbs gently, with the heathery height of Great Calva away to your right, and the lower but no less heathery mound of Little Calva directly ahead.

Across the watershed, Dash Beck on your left grows in stature with every stride, the track leading you down to a bridge that crosses it just above the spectacular Dash Falls, also known as Whitewater Dash. Through a gate the falls appear on your right, with the fertile land around Orthwaite and Binsey spreading before you.

Now all that remains is to follow the access road out to the Orthwaite road and there turn left to return to your starting point in about twenty minutes.

Start/Finish Lay-by, along the Orthwaite road, GR 235295

Distance 19km (11³/₄ miles)

Height gain 990m (3248ft)

Walking time 6-6¹/₂ hours

Type of walk A high and demanding mountain walk with little protection against bad weather but capable of being followed in poor visibility, guided by fencelines

The Route in Brief

Start From the lay-by, locate gate/stile and follow pathways across fields to track at entrance to Southerndale.

1 Descend to cross Southerndale Beck and cross ridge into Barkbethdale.

2 Go R, ascending sledgate, and follow path round on to Broad End.

3 Turn R, and ascend across Broad End, North Col and North Top, to summit.

4 Continue S, across undulating rocky summits to gate/fence.

5 Follow fence on to Little Man.

6 Follow fence again to cross main trail, continuing along fenceline/wall to Lonscale Fell, and east top.

7 Descend steeply to reach Burnt Horse, and main valley track to Skiddaw House.

8 Follow broad track from Skiddaw House past Dash Falls to Orthwaite road, there turning L to reach start.

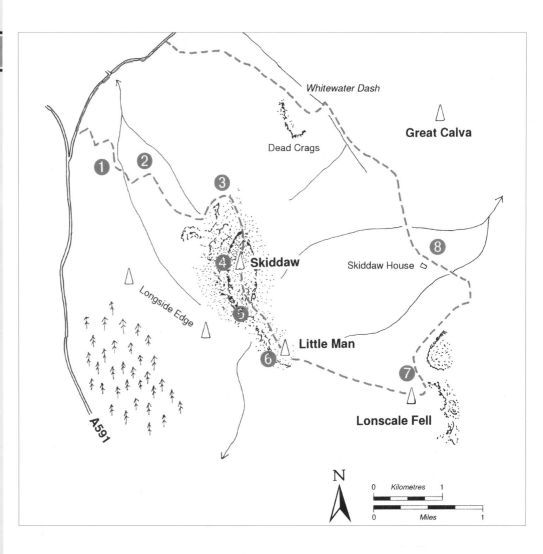

GREAT CALVA, KNOTT AND GREAT COCKUP

Thanks to a massive fault line that extends southwards through Glenderaterra and the Vale of Thirlmere, travellers along the Penrith to Keswick road gain an alluring glimpse of a purple pyramid positioned at precisely the point where the great down-sweeping lines of Blencathra and Lonscale Fell meet. But for this geological happenstance few visitors to Lakeland would know Great Calva, for that is its name, exists. Yet, in spite of lying at the heart of a superb moorland region, Great Calva receives scant attention from walkers, and its bouldery summit, perfectly set for quiet contemplation, contents itself with just a few, discerning, passers-by.

The finest approach uses an old supply road (a public bridleway) leading to Skiddaw House Youth Hostel. Almost opposite Peter House Farm along the Orthwaite road, a gate gives access to this rough but surfaced road, which leads initially through gated farm-land pastures before branching to Dash Farm. As you walk, the white exclamation mark of Dash Falls (Whitewater Dash) pinpoints your immediate objective. When the supply road drops towards Dash Beck, bear right and follow the track past the spectacular cascades, and up above them, to cross a small bridge, beyond which the trail, here part of the Cumbria Way, speeds on towards Skiddaw House.

Not far beyond Dash Falls **(1)** the track reaches a high point and from it you can ascend left over heather and grass on to the broad expanse of Little Calva. When a dilapidated fence is met, follow this to the cairn that marks the top of Little Calva, and then onwards through often boggy terrain to reach the northerly and highest of Great Calva's two summits **(2)**, amid a surprising rash of boulders and rock outcrops. The southerly summit boasts a small shelter from which the secrets of this wild moorland may be observed in peace and quiet.

The continuation to Knott is ill-advised in

Looking north from beside Dash Falls

Storm brewing over Great Calva and Knott

other than good visibility since there are few identifying features or well-trodden pathways to aid what could be difficult navigation.

There are certainly no rights of way until you meet the bridleway below Great Cockup, though the presence of considerate walkers is generally accepted.

On a fine day retreat along the old fenceline until you reach the point at which it bends abruptly, and from here head north to a narrow grassy col linking the Calva pair with Knott. With this invariably wet destination beneath your feet, head north-east across terrain quite featureless save for a solitary, and tantalising, cairn. As the gradient eases and the bald pate of Knott hoves into view so, too, do you see the true summit cairn, easily reached across short-cropped turf.

Knott **(3)** is the highest summit of the Uldale and Caldbeck Fells and stretches almost 5km (3 miles) from Coomb Height to Burn Tod. In good weather it proves to be just one of many delectable summits that provide excellent walking, wet in places and well suited to developing the skills of map and compass work that will be needed here and elsewhere in Lakeland in poorer conditions.

The linking col with Great Sca Fell is seldom dry and not easy to locate immediately. Its summit is marked by a modest cairn, smaller in stature than that on adjacent Little Sca Fell, by way of which the neat lump of Meal Fell can be reached.

Beyond Meal Fell **(4)** lies Great Cockup, the start of a long descending ridge that will return you to the Orthwaite road. But first you encounter the gap of Trusmadoor, a natural pass through the hills. From Great Cockup **(5)**, reached by an easy pull up grassy slopes, you can follow its natural line westwards, over Little Cockup, before descending south to meet a bridleway, and so walk out to the road **(6)**. Once there, not far from Orthwaite, turn left and simply follow the road back to your starting point. This (usually) quiet back lane is at its best in early spring, when the hedgerows are filled with flowers, breeding birds come and go in search of food and the pastures bleat loudly with the sound of new life.

FACT FILE

Start/Finish Lay-by along Orthwaite road, GR 249323
Distance 15km (9¹/₂ miles)
Height gain 800m (2625ft)
Walking time 5-6 hours
Type of walk Mainly grassy, but often wet. Once the supply road is left there are few continuous and clearly defined pathways, making this a walk for a clear day

The Route in Brief
Start From the lay-by follow the Skiddaw House supply road to its high point above Dash Falls.
1 Leave the road and climb on to Little Calva, following fenceline to Great Calva.
2 Retreat along fence and then bear off to linking col with Knott, and ascend from there.
3 Follow wide grassy ridges over Great Sca Fell, Little Sca Fell and Meal Fell.
4 Descend to cross Trusmadoor and climb on to Great Cockup.
5 Follow descending ridge to Little Cockup, and then drop S to intersect bridleway running out to Orthwaite road.
6 Follow road back to starting point.

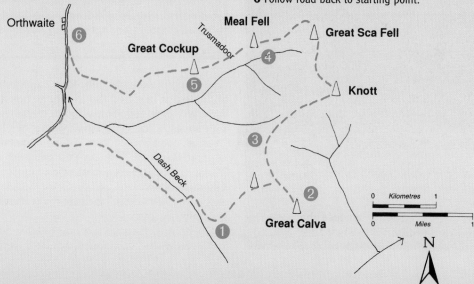

BOWSCALE FELL, BANNERDALE CRAGS AND SOUTER FELL

Beside the River Glenderamackin with Bannerdale Crags behind

Behind the great ridged bulk of Blencathra, the grassy heights of Bowscale Fell, Bannerdale Crags and haunted Souter Fell by comparison receive only a modest share of attention from walkers. Yet from the village of Mungrisdale, where the River Glenderamackin performs a U-turn *en route* to the River Derwent, the ascent of these outliers makes a fine undertaking, especially on a clear day in winter.

From Mungrisdale, start along the narrow lane past the telephone box and through a gate, following a rough track heading towards the pyramidal shape of The Tongue, which proves to be an elongated spur of Bowscale Fell. As you progress, so Bannerdale Crags comes into view across the Glenderamackin.

A short way beyond the gate the track dips to cross a stream by a bridge (1). From here ascend an obvious track around the southern slopes of The Tongue, climbing steadily until the track forks at a small collapsed cairn. Here the track on the left is more prominent and leads into Bannerdale, once the scene of lead-mining activity. Ignore this and step up, right, to pursue a grassy ramp that rises arrow-straight to the rim of the escarpment ahead. As you climb, so the profile of Bannerdale Crags becomes ever more striking. The obvious east ridge, directly across Bannerdale, is an alternative route to the summit for energetic walkers and easily reached from the bridge mentioned earlier.

Continue ahead on reaching the wide grassy col linking Bowscale Fell with Bannerdale Crags until, at a small collapsed cairn, you reach a crosspath (2). Here, turn right and stroll up a wide grassy trod to the stone shelter on the summit. A large cairn, lower in height, stands a short distance to the east.

The view from Bowscale Fell is quite outstanding. Far to the east you can see Cross Fell and the Dun Fells, the highest summits of the Pennines. Further north, on a good day you can pick out the Cheviots on the Anglo-Scottish border. Round to the north the Tweedsmuir Hills beyond Moffat rise into view, while much nearer loom the masses of Carrock Fell and High Pike. Beyond the latter you can see Criffel on the Solway Coast, and to its left, far, far away, the great heights of the Galloway Hills, rising to their highest summit, The Merrick. Within the immediate realm The Knott, Great Calva and Skiddaw all are displayed to good effect, while west of south the enormous bulk of Blencathra is a formidable challenge, rising above the broad expanse of Bannerdale Crags. Further south you can see the Dodds, Helvellyn and Fairfield, and to the south-east the fells that surround High Street beyond Patterdale.

From the summit **(3)** return to the cross-path and continue ahead (south), soon leaving the path and branching half left (south-east) to reach the edge of the escarpment above Bannerdale. In winter, this edge, away from the prevailing wind, retains a large mass of snow and forms a series of cornices that should be avoided. But a narrow path runs along above it in summer and leads directly to the conventional summit of Bannerdale Crags **(4)**, overlooking the dale below and Souter Fell, your next objective. The true summit, however, lies a short distance further east and provides a breathtaking view of the eastern slopes of Blencathra, of Foule Crag and Sharp Edge, set against the smooth bulk of Scales Fell.

From the top of Bannerdale Crags you may elect to return by your outward route, but otherwise head north-west and then west to reach the col linking with Foule Crag and Blencathra. Two streams flow away either side of the col, north-west and south-east. The former flows into the River Caldew, which finds its way east to the River Eden and

Skiddaw and Lonscale Fell from the summit of Bowscale Fell

the Solway Firth, while the latter is the infant River Glenderamackin and joins the River Derwent heading west.

Leave the col **(5)** heading south-east and take a descending path on the north side of

25

FACT FILE

Start/Finish Mungrisdale, GR 362303. Limited roadside parking near telephone box and along approach road to village
Distance 11½km (7 miles)
Height gain 650m (2130ft)
Walking time 5 hours
Type of walk Predominantly grassy, usually with a discernible path. Not to be attempted in poor visibility. Winter risk of cornices on Bannerdale Crags

The Route in Brief

Start Leave Mungrisdale village along the track beside the telephone box, and continue to cross stream by footbridge.

1 Ascend from bridge keeping round the base of The Tongue, and at fork, branch R and climb to col.

2 At crosspath turn R (N) and walk up to Bowscale Fell.

3 Retrace steps to crosspath. Continue ahead and soon branch L, leaving path, to reach edge above Bannerdale. Follow path to summit of fell.

4 Head west to highest point, and then NW to reach col at head of Glenderamackin.

5 Descend along course of Glenderamackin, later crossing it by a footbridge and climbing to col above Mousthwaite Comb.

6 Go E, and NE across tussock grass on to Souter Fell and continue NE along top of fell, before descending steeply to Mungrisdale.

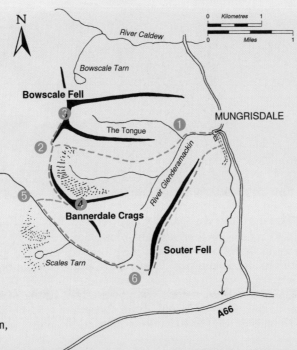

the Glenderamackin which later drops towards the river. Cross the river by a footbridge and climb the opposite side to a neck of land above Mousthwaite Comb **(6)**. Walkers wanting to omit Souter Fell should not cross the footbridge, but continue along the track above the Glenderamackin, to be led unerringly, if circuitously, back to Mungrisdale village.

From the col, head initially east and then north-east over trackless tussock grass to reach the higher ground of Souter Fell, formed into a series of bumps, and continue to the cairn composed of large boulders that marks the highest point.

Souter Fell in spite of its modest proportions has an enormous reputation among those who record spectral occurrences, for here on Midsummer Eve in 1735 a farm servant saw the whole of the eastern side of the mountain covered with marching troops coming from the northern end and disappearing near the summit. It was ten years and many derogatory remarks later before enough witnesses – twenty six in all – came forward to attest to this and other similar apparitions before a magistrate. In spite of so many reliable witnesses to the same event, no mark was found on the ground of footprints, hoofs or carriage tracks, or of any passage whatsoever.

Continue along the Souter Fell top, gradually and then steeply descending through bracken to reach Mungrisdale behind the Mill Inn.

BLENCATHRA BY HALL'S FELL RIDGE AND DODDICK FELL

There is wide consensus among aficionados of Lakeland walking that the ascent of Blencathra by Hall's Fell Ridge is one of *the* finest, if not the finest, route to the summit of any of the Lake District fells. This invigorating approach has fine views not only of the ultimate objective, to which it leads directly, and of the adjoining fells and ridges, but of the Dodds to the south and the fells that rise above Borrowdale and the Newlands valley. Combining this ascent with a descent of another splendid ridge, Doddick Fell, proves to be a most exhilarating excursion, one that in winter conditions calls, in places, for all the skills and expertise one might expect of an Alpine climber.

The ascent begins in the village of Threlkeld, famed for its huntsmen, many of whom are named and remembered on a monument in the churchyard. Threlkeld

Near the top of Doddick Fell

Blencathra: Upper Hall's Fell Ridge

As you walk on, suddenly a stunning view appears of Hall's Fell Top rising above the as-yet-unseen recesses of Gate Gill. The path leads to another gate, with a bench close by, and beyond bears right, across Gate Gill, in the vicinity of the disused Woodend lead mine (2).

Once across the stream, start up a steeply ascending path that manoeuvres through bracken, heather and low rock outcrops to gain a foothold on the broad base of Hall's Fell Ridge. The route is never in doubt and frequent, much-needed rest halts will allow you to take in the verdant richness of the valley fields below and the ever-widening panorama of Great and Little Mell Fells and the blue-green fells around Derwent Water.

After what seems like a long haul, the gradient eases as the ridge begins to narrow, at first only marginally and then more dramatically as Doddick Fell and the bulkier Scales Fell come into view. A wide outcrop of rock spanning the width of the ridge marks the start of the section known as Narrow Edge, a succession of shapely outcrops, mini-towers, gullies and ledges that walkers adept at scrambling will find delightful to tackle head on. Less confident walkers will find a means of escape for much of the ascent on one side or other of the ridge, though in the end it becomes easier to deal with the ridge than to try avoiding it.

The great beauty of the ridge is that it leads unerringly to the summit (3), marked by a countersunk OS trig station and a collapsed

is now bypassed by the A66, but soon after leaving this busy road, turn right on a minor back road that continues to a public bridleway on the left (a farm access marked 'Private Road' on a gate pillar), leading up to Gategill Farm (1). As you reach the farm, go ahead through a gate into the farmyard, passing between buildings to a double gate that gives on to an enclosed pathway above the neat ravine and cascades of Gate Gill.

cairn of modest proportions set amid a bald patch in an otherwise grassy expanse. The view, not surprisingly, is outstanding and reaches far into the heart of Lakeland as well as northwards and north-west to the lower Northern Fells and Skiddaw.

The continuation to Doddick Fell bears right (north-east) following a broad path and the escarpment above Doddick Gill. When, at a small cairn, this path forks, go right and continue descending, an attractive array of rock turrets delineating the right-hand edge. To the left, Sharp Edge eases into view above unseen Scales Tarn, while beyond this hiatus rise the mounds of Bannerdale Crags and Bowscale Fell.

The descending path continues to Scales Fell, probably the easiest way down, but *en route* it becomes possible to move right on a narrow trod leading to the crags at the top of Doddick Fell (4). The start of the way down Doddick Fell takes to a narrow shaly path flirting with rock outcrops, maintaining a steepness that calls for caution for some way down the ridge. The whole of this upper section may be avoided by staying on the Scales Fell path for a little longer, to reach a cairn that marks the upper limit of a more regular path sliding across the fellside to meet the main Doddick ridge beneath the most awkward section.

The continuation down the ridge is a pleasure to walk. It gives fine views of Clough Head and Great Dodd and Hall's Fell Top in particular, as it passes through a mantle of heather before reaching a final outcrop immediately beyond which the ridge broadens and plummets to the buildings and green pastures of Doddick Farm.

The route now moves right, descending gradually to reach the intake wall (5) not far east of Doddick Gill. Follow the path, right, alongside the wall and when it starts to move away towards the gill, stay with the wall to its end, there turning left to drop down to cross the gill at a ford. A good path leads on then above the on-going intake wall and pleasantly across the base of Hall's Fell Ridge back to Gate Gill near the Woodend mine, from where you simply retrace your outward steps.

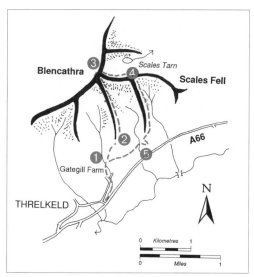

FACT FILE

Start/Finish Threlkeld village, GR 325255
Distance 6km (3³/₄ miles)
Height gain 720m (2362ft)
Walking time 3-4 hours
Type of walk Steep, demanding start followed by a long section of scrambling. The descent is also steep, and can be tiring. Dangerous and difficult in winter conditions

The Route in Brief
Start Leave Threlkeld along back road and track to Gategill Farm.
1 Pass through farmyard to cross Gate Gill near disused mine.
2 Ascend broad base of ridge and follow ridge to summit.
3 Go NE and soon fork R, descending to top of Doddick Fell.
4 Follow ridge path down to intake wall.
5 Cross Doddick Gill and follow path above intake wall to Gategill Farm. Retrace outward steps from there.

BLENCATHRA BY SHARP EDGE

Ascending Sharp Edge

Travellers entering the Lake District along the A66 from Penrith will see most graphically why Blencathra, the first significant mountain they will encounter, also bears the (less imaginative) name of Saddleback, for, like a saddle, the summit plateau dips across the corrie basin that houses Scales Tarn before rising again to the top of Sharp Edge. It is by this edge, a narrow, naked, airy arête, that this walk goes, and provides walkers with a fine and entertaining scramble. The ascent is enhanced by a steady walk-in from the A66, ascending first through Mousthwaite Comb before paralleling the course of the River Glenderamackin to reach Scales Tarn.

Begin along the minor road (which is signposted Souter Fell) just east of the White Horse Inn and follow it until you start to descend to the bridge spanning Comb Beck. Here **(1)**, leave the road and ascend left to a stile and continue along the edge of a field to gain a conspicuous rising track curling round the flanks of Mousthwaite Comb. As you leave the comb **(2)**, head initially south of west towards Scales Fell on a grassy track to a meeting of pathways. Here turn right on a path travelling high above the Glenderamackin **(3)** until it meets Scales Beck, a normally gushing stream flowing down from the left. Cross the beck and ascend along its banks to the sanctuary of Scales Tarn **(4)**.

In *The Bridal of Triermain*, Sir Walter Scott, although mistakenly calling Blencathra Glaramara, observes:

The surface of that sable tarn,
in whose black mirror you may spy
The stars, while noontide lights the sky.

The tarn also has a reputation for being the coldest in Lakeland because, as Harriet Martineau described in 1855, it 'is so situated at the foot of a vast precipice, and so buried among crags, that the sun never reaches it, except through a crevice in early morning'. It is a powerful setting, so awesome that one early traveller 'wished to lose blood and return', while another 'was seen through the mists lying prostrate on the ground'.

From the tarn ascend a steeply rising path to gain the end of Sharp Edge. The onward route keeps to the Edge itself, across which the way has been polished by countless pairs of boots, though there is an escape path on the north side of the Edge by means of which the principal difficulties may be avoided. In winter conditions, Sharp Edge can give a brief taste of alpinism at its best and requires the use of crampons and also an ice axe.

Once the top of Sharp Edge is reached, follow a good path left for the short walk to the summit cairn, passing on the way the branching descent to Scales Fell and Doddick Fell.

On leaving the summit (5), retreat to the start of the descent to Scales Fell, a prominent track branching at a small cairn, and go down, following the path beyond the top of Doddick Fell (6) and on to cross the grassy top of Scales Fell. Here the path becomes less obvious, but your aim is to descend towards the top of Mousthwaite Comb. Along the way you will rejoin your outward route (7) above the River Glenderamackin, when you can either retrace your steps through Mousthwaite Comb, or turn right along a prominent path that leads you around Scales Fell to a gate through which a brief descent leads you on to the A66, a short distance west of your starting point at the White Horse Inn.

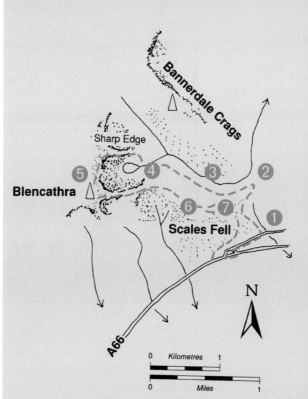

FACT FILE

Start/Finish White Horse Inn, GR 343269. Limited roadside parking along A66
Total distance 8km (5 miles)
Height gain 655m (2150ft)
Walking time 4-5 hours
Type of walk Generally a straightforward route, but involving moderate scrambling, made difficult by high winds

The Route in Brief

Start Leave the A66, near the White Horse Inn and follow back road until you can leave it by a stile, **before** crossing Comb Beck.
1 Ascend through Mousthwaite Comb to col.
2 Go L (S of W) to join Scales Fell path and turn R on good path above Glenderamackin.
3 Cross Scales Beck and ascend, L, to Scales Tarn.
4 Climb steeply on to Sharp Edge and follow ridge upwards. (Easier path on N side.) At top of ascent go left on good path to summit.
5 Retreat to start of descent to Scales Fell, and follow path down, crossing top of Doddick Fell en route.
6 Continue across Scales Fell and descend towards top of Mousthwaite Comb, as far as meeting of paths.
7 Either retrace steps, or go R at junction to follow path out to A66, W of White Horse Inn.

2

THE DERWENT FELLS

Feeding the River Derwent, and in due course the River Cocker, the Derwent Fells embrace two distinct upland areas. One, sometimes known as the North Western Fells, forms a catchment around Coledale Beck; the other around Newlands and Keskadale Becks, and known as the Newlands Fells.

Forming two great and independent ridges, the fells of the north-west rise to their greatest at the head of Coledale on Crag Hill, reaching then northwards to take in the shapely cone of Grisedale Pike. The complete round of the Coledale watershed is an outstanding tour, one of the finest combined ridge walks in Lakeland. In spite of their limited extent, the Newlands Fells also possess two splendid ridges, perfect for walking and a comely collection of summits.

Lying south-west of Derwent Water and with a substantial foothold in Buttermere, this compact region is one of the smallest in the Lake District and an ideal arena both for tyros and regular walkers alike.

The profile of the fells, characteristically smooth-sided, betrays the underlying Skiddaw

Beside the River Derwent at Grange

Slates and bears a vegetation mainly of grass, bracken and heather. Here and there heady-perfumed gorse bushes lend an aromatic air to many walks, while elsewhere farms sit tidily amid neatly quartered fields bordered with willow, ash, sycamore and oak. Red squirrels and a wide variety of birds provide finishing touches to a pastoral masterpiece, vibrantly verdant in spring and summer, tawny with coppery bracken and withering grasses in autumn.

Yet it has not escaped the attentions of those who sought wealth within the Lakeland fells. At Goldscope, beneath the craggy brows of High Spy and Dale Head, man has mined for copper since the thirteenth century. Yielding also lesser quantities of lead, silver and gold, it is not surprising that the mine became known as Gottesgab, or God's Gift, so appearing in records in 1569.

The sixteenth century saw the greatest period of mining activity in Newlands, when Elizabeth I brought miners from Germany and encouraged increased production by the granting of royal patronage and the waiving of taxes as a form of hidden subsidy. Ore was taken from the mines by packhorse to the shores of Derwent Water and from there to bloomeries on the banks of the River Greta at Brigham. The copper was then given the Queen's mark at the Receiving House in Keswick, now the Moot Hall.

Newlands lies along the northern fringe of the ancient Copeland Forest and was first colonised at the end of the Middle Ages. It has a remarkable individuality in spite of its lack of a lake or the highly dramatic qualities formed from rocks of the Borrowdale Volcanic Series. To a very large extent it has escaped, even today, the impact of tourism and so lacks many of the Victorian-inspired plantations and buildings that ring the shores of Derwent Water.

Across Newlands Hause, where the foothills of Robinson meet the idyllic Knott Rigg, the road descends steeply to the valley of Buttermere, encountering first the village church perched on a rocky knoll overlooking the main group of buildings that comprise the community.

In this brief compass, the diligent walker can pass many enjoyable days of quality walking, striding lofty ridges between high peaks or exploring some of the most lovely of Lakeland valleys. This is not a scene of which one ever tires.

THE COLEDALE HORSESHOE

The satisfaction that flows from a long day high among the hills is perfectly generated on this round of the Coledale valley, on which you instantly rise to a lofty ridge of summits in quick succession and continue in much the same vein throughout the walk. A bright clear day will only serve to heighten the experience. In winter an ice axe will be needed, and possibly crampons in one or two places.

Start from the bridge at Stonycroft near the village of Stair, and follow a rising path across the flanks of Rowling End to the col between that outlying summit and the shapely cone of Causey Pike.

The knobbly profile of Causey Pike is a distinctive picture-postcard backdrop to the town of Keswick and a useful guide in locating other, less easily identified summits in the confusing array of the Derwent Fells. Strong walkers can begin by ascending Rowling End.

Beyond the col, the final pull to the summit of Causey Pike is rocky and delightful and though it will require the use of hands near the top, need deter no one.

Once the summit (1) is reached, the long ridge to Crag Hill springs into view, undulating into the distance and an exciting prospect. Keep along the ridge to the next summit, Scar Crags (not to be confused with Scar Crag further on, the southern face of Crag Hill).

The top of Scar Crags is rather uninteresting, beyond which the path drops to a grassy col from which an escape route flows back, south of Outside, to Braithwaite or Stonycroft. As you descend to the col the slopes ahead of Sail appear more severe than they prove to be. The prominent path misses the highest point of Sail, to which you should divert briefly.

The final section of this southern part of the circuit rises to Crag Hill (2), a summit with an identity crisis, for it has long been known as Eel Crag, though this properly applies to the crags on the northern face of the mountain. To add to the confusion, maps differ on the naming of the fell. Whatever you call it, the ascent from Sail is exhilarating, but woefully brief. You descend from Sail to a narrow link with the higher

Left: Grisedale Pike
Opposite: Hobcarton Crags

summit, before scampering easily up a narrow crest to the summit trig.

Directly west lies the enormous bulk of Grasmoor, but though Crag Hill is lower, it is a far better summit, placed centrally to these fells and with outstanding views, if you take the trouble to explore the summit plateau.

Your next objective, Coledale Hause, is a high mountain pass at the head of Coledale Beck and Lisa Beck, and a confusing place in mist. It lies west of north from Crag Hill and a direct descent can be made, but leads into an abomination of loose scree and rocks that can so easily be avoided by setting off west towards the col with Grasmoor, there turning northwards on a good path, beside the upper branch of Lisa Beck, bound for Coledale Hause **(3)**.

FACT FILE

Start/Finish Stonycroft, GR 232213
Distance 14km (8¾ miles)
Height gain 1110m (3640ft)
Walking time 4-5 hours
Type of walk High level ridge walking generally on good paths throughout

The Route in Brief

Start From Stonycroft ascend across flank of Rowling End to col below Causey Pike, and from there to the summit.
1 Continue along ridge over Scar Crags and Sail to connecting ridge to Crag Hill (Eel Crags).
2 Descend W to broad col, and N to Coledale Hause.
3 Climb obliquely to ridge above Hobcarton Crags.
4 Go R, along dilapidated wall, over intermediate summit and on to Grisedale Pike.
5 Descend long ridge, Sleet How, to Braithwaite village.
6 Go through village, and above woodland, to rejoin back road to Stonycroft.

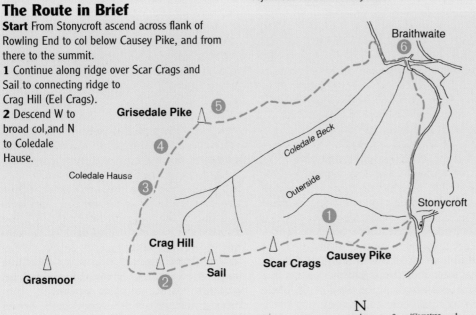

An escape route from Coledale lies east, through old mine workings below Force Crag, and from Coledale Hause this is the most prominent of paths. Take care then to locate the path **(4)** for Grisedale Pike, slanting north-east to Grisedale Pike's unnamed companion (south-west of the main summit), where you encounter a dilapidated wall beyond which lie the spectacular Hobcarton Crags, too friable to interest rock gymnasts, but of great appeal to passing walkers and botanists. The onward ascent of Grisedale Pike is obvious, rising steadily to a slaty summit **(5)** that can prove slippery when wet.

All that then remains is to descend by the Pike's north-west ridge, Sleet How. Great care is needed immediately on leaving the summit, where erosion has taken its toll and the steep slaty path justifies caution. Once Sleet How is reached, the difficulties ease, and the path runs on easily down to Braithwaite **(6)**, finishing a short way north of the village.

Walk down to the village and turn right on the back road that runs to Stair and Stonycroft. Cross a bridge spanning Coledale Beck, continue ahead and, at a bend, leave the road for a track that goes towards Braithwaite Lodge, continuing beyond the Lodge and above a small area of woodland to re-emerge on the back road about 1 km (a little over ½ a mile) north of your starting point at Stonycroft.

AROUND THE NEWLANDS VALLEY

Not until the mid-nineteenth century did the persistently Philistine view of Lakeland which had long pervaded the English aristocracy start to change – mountains meant bad roads, poor accommodation, if any, the fear of being robbed and the prospect, very real, of losing one's way. In this respect Lakeland was little different from the other mountainous regions of Britain, and likewise was seldom visited, at least until the adventurous Victorians came on the scene, seeking out the terrors and splendours of the place.

One such place of splendour, for it could never have been conceived as a place of terror, was the Newlands valley, encircled by one of the smallest groups of fells in the Lake District. Lying south-west of Derwent Water, these fine groups of fells boast two splendid ridges, roughly at right angles, and a fine selection of shapely summits. The underlying rocks, Skiddaw Slates, betray themselves in the characteristic smooth shape of the fells, the general absence of tarns and a vegetation mainly of grass and heather.

This round of the Newlands valley takes in all but one of the principal fells overlooking Buttermere and begins from near Rigg Beck where a disused quarry has been turned to good car parking advantage. From here you set off up the road, soon turning left to pursue quiet lanes leading to your first objective, Newlands Chapel. Take the track on the left, just past the chapel, and follow this to Low Snab Farm (1).

Along this initial section the true beauty of the Newlands valley becomes apparent; farms sit prettily in the middle of neatly patterned fields dotted with sheep and bordered with willow, ash, sycamore and oak. The red squirrel can be found here sharing the tree tops with jays, thrushes, cuckoos, pipits and a variety of tits – great, blue, long-tailed, coal and willow.

Ahead lies Hindscarth, the 'Pass of the Deer', the shapeliest of summits, its great tilted peak and attendant ridge starkly etched against the sky. There is a peaceful calm about the place that draws you on, beyond the farm, and through a gate to gain the open fellside. Immediately to hand are the waste spills of the Goldscope Mine, another section of which can be seen, left, across the valley.

Goldscope was one of Lakeland's most prosperous mines, its name first appearing in records in 1569 as 'Gottesgab' or 'God's Gift'. Here copper was mined as early as the thirteenth century from a vein 2.75m (9ft) thick. Large amounts of lead, too, were found, a small amount of silver, and, so it is said, a modicum of gold. It is possible to venture into the mine which enters beneath Scope End, but it is wet underfoot, low in places, dangerous and quite black inside!

Follow the wall behind Low Snab Farm for a short distance and then ascend left to gain Scope End. The going is a little stiff, but there is a clear path and when the initial pull is completed, and with the whole ridge to Hindscarth stretching before you, the splendour of the situation easily overcomes any weariness; in any case there are many places to rest for a while.

Continue along the ridge. It narrows in a few places, but never threateningly so, with a path that cavorts up and down, switching from one side of the ridge to the other, until you arrive at the foot of the final haul to the summit. A steady plod is required, and in spite of its initially daunting appearance, you soon find yourself beside the cairn which has been prominent throughout your approach – a circular shelter, in fact – beyond which, a short distance, lies the true summit, marked by a modest cairn in the middle of a stony plateau.

Press on from the summit **(2)** along a cairned path leading south to a small prominence on which appears the occasional remnant of an old fenceline and a clear pathway. Turn right here and descend to a col, before ascending again, this time along a new fenceline, to a large cairn. Now you must turn north across stony ground to reach the summit of Robinson, a fine fell named after a local worthy, Richard Robinson, who, quick to perceive the opportunities afforded by the Dissolution of the Monasteries, purchased it during the reign of Henry VIII.

From the summit of Robinson **(3)** you should head a little south of west and descend to Buttermere Moss, a rather boggy place but not too trying, unless you persist in going after prolonged wet weather. Your target is Moss Force, where Moss Beck descends abruptly to Newlands Hause. Cross the beck and you will soon encounter a safe path down to the west side of the falls, initially difficult to locate (don't attempt to follow the falls down). It calls for a little care, but the level ground at the top of the Hause **(4)** is soon reached, and, pressing on a short distance from the car fumes, you can rest and gaze down on the distant beauty that is Buttermere.

Anyone now feeling tired should retreat to Rigg Beck by the roadway, but otherwise tackle the slopes of Knott Rigg, which can be trying. Once on the highest ground, stay there, avoiding the spur (right) which descends to Keskadale and continue headily along a splendid ridge running onwards over Ard Crags and down by Aikin Knott to reach the intake wall and the road near Birkrigg, from where the car park at Rigg Beck is but a few minutes' stroll.

Above the Newlands valley

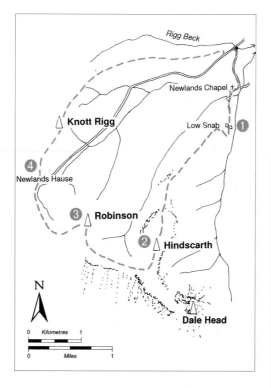

FACT FILE

Start/Finish Small parking spot near Rigg Beck, GR 229202
Distance 12km (7½ miles)
Height gain 1010m (3310ft)
Walking time Allow 4-5 hours
Type of walk Only in a few places is this walk energetic – the start up Scope End, the pull to Hindscarth summit, the modest ascent to Robinson and the final ascent to Knott Rigg. The descent by Moss Beck to Newlands Hause calls for care and attention. At all other times it represents a delightful excursion, suitable for most regular walkers of all ages, except the very young

The Route in Brief
Start From a small quarry parking place near Rigg Beck head for Newlands Chapel, there turning L to reach Low Snab Farm.
1 Continue on to the ridge leading up to Hindscarth.
2 From the summit keep in same direction to reach dilapidated fence and follow this R, first descending and then climbing to summit of Robinson.
3 Descend across Buttermere Moss to follow path beside Moss Force to Newlands Hause. Path requires care.
4 Cross road and ascend Knott Rigg, following ridge (avoid right branching spur) over Ard Crags and descend to rejoin road near Rigg Beck.

CAT BELLS, HIGH SPY AND CASTLE CRAG

Many a first, faltering step to fell-walking freedom was planted on the grassy slopes of Cat Bells, sparking the flame of affection that grows in intensity as each new summit of these delectable hills is achieved, each new valley explored. Few will not be moved by the remarkable panorama from the top of Cat Bells, and fewer still will never return, for Cat Bells holds enormous appeal.

Yet Cat Bells is but the northern end of a fine ridge, flanked by steep, craggy slopes falling to exceptional valleys, both of which provide good walking for the return journey. To the west lies a branch of the Newlands valley, culminating at Dale Head, while to the east the River Derwent carves a course through the much-loved valley of Borrowdale. This walk returns through Borrowdale in order to visit Castle Crag – the renowned tooth in the jaws of Borrowdale – but those in search of a quieter interlude in their day will find the Newlands valley route, accessed from close by Dalehead Tarn, perfectly fits the bill.

Begin from Hawes End, where the road from Swinside and Portinscale makes a sharp zigzag before easing round the side of Cat Bells. Just above the hairpin bend, a path can be seen rising sharply up the fellside. Follow this through all its minor deviations, climbing steadily through grass and bracken to encounter a few small rocky outcrops before reaching the lower, northernmost summit of Cat Bells, sometimes called Brandlehow. Onward, the way is never in doubt – a broad trail keeping to the centre of a grassy ridge before rising dramatically through more rock outcrops to the cone of Cat Bells, a rocky top-knot and a splendid objective. In one or two places the path moves close to the grassy slopes which will be slippery when wet and so a little care is needed until the summit **(1)** is reached.

The view from this modest height is outstanding. The great expanse of Derwent Water lies directly below, while to the north the slaty slopes of Skiddaw, Little Man and Carl Side soar above the market town of Keswick. Further right, the southern ridges of Blencathra cling to Glenderamackin Vale, while its northern rump sits firmly on the vast

heatherlands of Mungrisdale Common and the gathering grounds of the Caldew. To the east the Dodds lead into the Helvellyn range, while to the west lofty fells tumble across the skyline in endless profusion from Lord's Seat, across Grisedale Pike and Eel Crags to the high ground above unseen Buttermere and to Robinson, Hindscarth and Dale Head.

Beyond Cat Bells the great bulk of Maiden Moor, rising from the walls of Little Town in the Newlands valley, invites you on. The initial descent from Cat Bells involves negotiating its rocky aureole before you are free to stride purposefully towards Hause Gate, a broad grassy col linking the two summits.

Now tackle the slopes of Maiden Moor ahead, a series of stepped rises that terminate in a grassy top **(2)**. The main path skips around the highest point, to which a diversion is well-advised, to gaze down upon the loveliness of Newlands set against the backdrop of the smooth-flanked North Western Fells. Return to the path and follow its unerring

Along the Cat Bells ridge

course to the fine handiwork of the substantial cairn on the top of High Spy. *En route* the steep sides of Hindscarth and Dale Head in particular hold your attention and you can excite your progress by keeping close (but not too close!) to the edge above the concealed Eel Crags that fall into Newlands. But as you reach the highest point of High Spy (3) your focus is drawn south to the mighty Scafell group and Great Gable, and the immediate bulk of Dale Head.

From the summit, set off west of south on a descending rocky path, heading towards the glint of Dalehead Tarn on the col below the fell. Long before reaching the tarn, however, you can branch left, passing Wilson's Bield to reach a fence near the top of Tongue Gill (4), an obvious broad gully on your left. Cross the shallow, in-flowing gill to reach a step stile, continuing beyond the fence on a path that crosses to the far side of the gully before descending to the disused Rigghead quarries. The quarries produced slate from levels cut deep into the fellside and a number of adits may still be entered, but they are dangerous, waterlogged and should not be explored beyond the penetration of daylight (if at all).

As the path descends so it reaches a first cluster of derelict quarry buildings, of fascination to anyone interested in industrial archaeology. Lower down more buildings can be seen and these are your objective: resist a tempting path branching left between the two main stands of buildings. Circle round the lower group and follow a broad access track down to cross Tongue Gill.

The track continues down the valley (5), now on the true left bank of Tongue Gill, passes through a gate and rounds a corner suddenly to face the tree-girt cone of Castle Crag. Continue along the approaching path as it leads close to the Crag and when a narrow path appears on the right leading to a wall, follow it over stiles to the top.

The Crag was given to the National Trust in 1920 by Sir William Hamer and his family in memory of their son, John Hamer, killed in action in 1918. Thomas West, author of *Antiquities of Furness*, and *A Guide to the Lakes* (which contained Thomas Gray's Journal) did much to influence visitors' attitudes to the Lake District, as they pursued more a fashionable necessity than a voyage of discovery. Of Castle Crag West wrote:

From the top of Castlecrag in Borrowdale, there is a most astonishing view of the lake and vale of Keswick, spread out to the north in the most picturesque manner ... a beautiful mixture of villages, houses, cots and farms, standing round the skirts of Skiddaw, which rises in the grandest manner from a verdant base and closes this prospect in the noblest style of nature's true sublime. From the summit of the rock the views are so singularly great and pleasing that they ought never to be omitted ...

Castle Crag, Borrowdale

This truly secreted spot is completely surrounded by the most horrid, romantic mountains that are in this region of wonders; and whoever omits this coup d'oeil hath probably seen nothing equal to it.

From the top of Castle Crag, much less a 'secreted spot' than when West visited it, return to the main track and follow this northwards (right) for a delectable encounter with the River Derwent at Gowder Dub. Continue north by an obvious path that eventually joins a metalled roadway. Go right here to reach the village of Grange **(6)** in a few minutes.

Turn left on reaching the road through Grange and follow this not-so-quiet back road as far as Manesty **(7)**, just beyond which you can leave the road (though you don't need to), and take a rising path, left, to a gate. Beyond the gate, a prominent path ascends to Hause Gate, but when the path forks, go right, to skirt above woodlands and Brackenburn, sometime home of Sir Hugh Walpole (1884-1941), the English novelist, born in Auckland, New Zealand, who bought the property in 1923. His collection of works known as *The Herries Chronicle* is set in and around Borrowdale.

Press on beyond Brackenburn, the path soon dipping to make a brief acquaintance with the road at a small quarry car park. Cross this gap and return to a fine path crossing the lower slopes of Cat Bells that will ultimately bring you back to Hawes End amid explosions of brightly hued, heady-scented gorse.

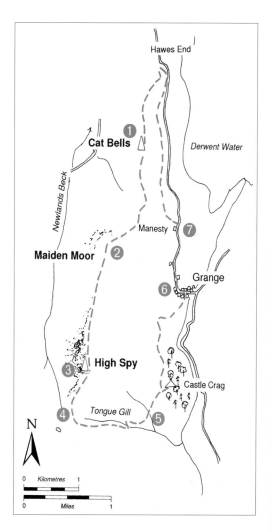

FACT FILE

Start/Finish Hawes End GR 247212
Distance 14½km (9 miles)
Height gain 875m (2870ft)
Walking time 4½-5 hours
Type of walk Very undulating, with height gain spread throughout the walk. Fine lofty ridge-walking on good paths, with a brief dip into industrial archaeology

The Route in Brief

Start From Hawes End locate path ascending on to the end of the Cat Bells ridge and follow obvious path to the summit.
1 Descend to Hause Gate and climb on to Maiden Moor.
2 Follow easy route across plateau to High Spy.
3 Descend towards Dalehead Tarn, but turn L halfway down to reach top of Tongue Gill.
4 Go down through quarries to reach broad trail at the bottom and turn L.
5 Head towards Castle Crag (up and down Crag), returning to main track, go R to Grange.
6 Turn L along road to Manesty.
7 Leave road, ascending slightly L, through gate and then R fork above woodland, returning on obvious path to Hawes End.

AROUND DERWENT WATER

In spite of its tenuous link with the Derwent Fells as such, this tour of Borrowdale's massive lake does nevertheless circumnavigate a major element in the flow of the River Derwent, but, more fundamentally, it is just too good a walk to miss. With some adjustments to allow for occasional (usually wintertime) flooding between Manesty Woods and Lodore and at the headland off Barrow House, the walk can be effected at any time of the year. It is especially pleasant on a cold, clear winter morning or early in springtime when the fields and hedgerows are bright with new life. Summer time launch services on the lake enable the journey to be curtailed at a number of points.

The walk begins in Keswick and may be followed in either direction, though it is described here anticlockwise. Start from the Moot Hall in the centre of Keswick. The Hall was built in 1813 on the site of an earlier building and was, until fairly recent times, used as the Town Hall. The word 'moot' means to argue or discuss, so the 'Moot Hall' was a place of discussion.

Leave Keswick along the main road, heading towards Cockermouth. Not far out of town the road crosses the River Greta and immediately afterwards you should turn left on to a footpath (signposted Portinscale). After about 60m/yd turn right, through a gate and follow a path across two fields to meet a road leading to Portinscale (1), at which you turn left. Cross a suspension bridge over the River Derwent and continue down the road to a T-junction and there again turn left.

After a little under ½ a mile (about 700km), the road bends sharply to the left and later to the right. At the right bend, go left down a lane to the lake (signposted Launch Pier). On reaching the lake turn right and go up past Nichol End marina to follow an obvious path past Fawe Park and the driveway to Lingholm (gate). Keep on through woodland and across fields on a path between fences. This eventually reaches another private driveway and when it does go left and shortly left again to reach Hawes End landing stage (2).

Derwent Water

Derwent Isle

At the lake turn right and follow the shore-line, cross a stile and pursue a fence to a section of boardwalks, continuing then by a pathway through pleasant woodland linking Low and High Brandlehow Piers.

Immediately after Brandlehow follow the path as it goes right, up steps. At the top, keep ahead to a small gate, beyond which you turn left towards a boathouse. Pass between huts to a gate and continue along a driveway, turning left on a path opposite a cottage (The Warren) **(3)**. Stay with the path to the shore and keep going to a gate in a wall in the middle of Manesty Woods. A short way on, ignore a footpath continuing to Grange and go left to another section of boardwalks leading to a gated bridge across the Derwent. Across the ensuing field you soon reach Borrowdale Road (4).

Go left along the road, past the Lodore Swiss Hotel until, about 200m/yd beyond Kettlewell car park you can turn left, over a stile to a shore path. You can follow this around the headland meeting the road again near Barrow House Youth Hostel and Ashness Gate pier.

Barrow House was built by an eccentric local, Joseph Pocklington, who used to live on Derwent Isle, but began building Barrow House in 1787. Known as Lord Pocky, he was responsible for annual regattas on Derwent Water and was described as a man of ebullient fancy who never understood the concept of restraint.

Keep on beyond Ashness Gate following the shore path. At Calfclose Bay the path then moves away from the road, with Rampsholme Island directly in front of you. As you follow the shoreline, the path comes to Stable Hills (5) where a right turn leads along the access road. Soon, however, go left, through a gate into woodland. Cross a footbridge and reach the shore again at another gate. The way is now clear, along the shoreline, to Friar's Crag (6), beyond which the path runs on into Hope Park and through a subway that brings you back into Keswick. Go up the street, left at the top, soon to return to the Moot Hall.

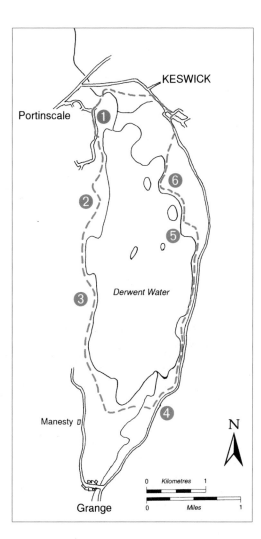

Start/Finish Moot Hall, Keswick, GR 266234
Distance 15km (9½ miles)
Height gain Nominal, but undulating
Walking time Allow 4½-5 hours
Type of walk Fairly easy walking, generally on good paths. Some flooding in wintertime, when you will have to take to the roads. Can be tiring towards the end

The Route in Brief
Start Leave Keswick on the Cockermouth road and just after crossing the River Greta go L on a footpath through fields and by back roads to Portinscale.
1 Half a mile after Portinscale go down lane to the lake and pass Nichol End marina, continuing to Hawes End.
2 Continue with shoreline to Brandlehow piers and keep on to reach a cottage called The Warren.
3 Go back to shoreline and through Manesty Woods, ignoring path to Grange, but going L to cross the River Derwent and reach Borrowdale road.
4 Turn L up road and after Kettlewell car park go over stile to another shore path that leads past Ashness Gate and on to Calfclose Bay and Stable Hills.
5 Soon turn L through gate into woodland, cross footbridge and rejoin shoreline, continuing to Friar's Crag.
6 Continue through Hope Park, and under subway to re-enter Keswick.

3

BUTTERMERE
AND THE VALE OF LORTON

Writing in 1929, in *Days in Lakeland: Past and Present*, E.M. Ward observed Buttermere to be:

...a dale very flowery and full of trees. The hesitant entry of spring into the vale of Buttermere is...troubled but by a cold nor'wester up the lakes or by the chill of a May snowfall on Red Pike and Great Gable...Across the dale near the end of Scale Bottom there is a dim pallor, of the same delicate hue as dew on flowering grasses, of the faint blue tinge that lies over screes in a clouded light.

It is, without question, one of the most endearing dales of Lakeland, brought to notoriety following the visit in 1792 of Captain Joseph Budworth who, in penning his experiences at the Fish Inn on finding the beautiful 'Maid of Buttermere', brought forth a deluge of idle and not-so-idle curiosity.

Yet there is far more to Buttermere and the Vale of Lorton than this moving tale, for the dale contains amazing variety, evidenced by the simple expedient of pursuing its river, the Cocker. In Walt Unsworth's view, 'All the scenic qualities for which Lakeland is justly famous are distilled

Grasmoor from Dodd (Red Pike)

and are concentrated in this area'. Perhaps only Borrowdale might compare, but few people would argue that Buttermere was not one of the most attractive of Lakeland dales.

From its birthplace on the steep sides of Dale Head, Honister Pass and Fleetwith Pike, the youthful stream, here called Gatesgarthdale Beck, pierces the austere, bouldery landscape contained within a classical U-shaped trough formed by post-glacial mountain debris that has modified the original V-shape. Across the hause at Honister, the streams flow down to the River Derwent and that will later combine with the River Cocker before flowing out to the sea.

At Gatesgarth, the valley broadens and levels. Here the infant river passes more serenely across an alluvial spread once covered by a much larger lake than the two remnants we see today. Beside the lake, great mountains rise steeply from its shores to the High Stile ridge and the moulded trinity of summits, Dale Head, Hindscarth and Robinson. Along the length of Buttermere as far as the village, the valley is uniformly contained by these flanking hills, and even beyond, to Hause Point, where the rocky buttress of Rannerdale Knots persists to the edge of Crummock Water.

Beyond, the dale opens out again, with only Grasmoor and Mellbreak crags offering any resistance before, at the far end of Crummock Water, the valley divides into the narrow dale containing Loweswater and the delectable Vale of Lorton, that so endeared itself to Wordsworth. The River Cocker, now much more assured following its journey through both Buttermere and Crummock Water, continues relentlessly northwards, eventually to join forces with the Derwent at Cockermouth.

Little distance has gone by from the head of the valley at Honister and Lorton Vale, but the contrast could not be greater between the bare bouldery landscape of the former and the lush meadows of Lorton.

Buttermere, with its two lakes, a village agreeably, almost smugly, set amid the mountains and the attractive cascade of Scale Force, has long been a popular tourist resort. That remains true and this compact stronghold plays an important role in the economy of the Lake District. And still maintains its air of charm and peacefulness. Its surrounding fells, as inspiring and striking as you will find in Lakeland and its many valley ways, provide days of wandering for walkers of all standards and ages.

WHITESIDE, HOPEGILL HEAD AND GASGALE GILL

The view of Whiteside from Lanthwaite Green is a daunting one; a steep, slaty scree path leads up through craggy ribs, holding little promise of respite. Yet this test of one's willpower brings a fine reward to those who pass it, for beyond lies a splendid, if woefully brief, ridge walk as good as any in Lakeland. With the added advantage of comparative neglect, and therefore greater solitude, this fine outing returns by way of Gasgale Gill, the scene on 9 September 1760 of wholesale devastation as a 'memorable water spout' descended on Grasmoor, sending tons of debris down the fellsides to fan out into the delta that today is Lanthwaite Green.

Cross the road from the car park and take to a green path heading for the foot of a minor satellite, Whin Ben. Cross the stream, Liza Beck (also called Gasgale Gill) and follow a path that starts work on Whin Ben.

The effort of ascent, first over Whin Ben

Opposite: The Whiteside Ridge

Above: Descending Gasgale Gill

51

Start/Finish Lanthwaite Green car park,
GR 158207
Distance 8km (5 miles)
Height gain 680m (2230ft)
Walking time 3-4 hours
Type of walk Initially strenuous ascent to
narrow ridge flanked by steep drops on one side,
but otherwise good walking

The Route in Brief

Start Leave the car park heading across
Lanthwaite Green and pursue path over Whin
Ben and steeply up to Whiteside.
1 Follow ridge to Hopegill Head.
2 Descend SE, then S over Sand Hill to Coledale
Hause.
3 Head roughly NW into head of Gasgale Gill
and follow path back to Lanthwaite Green.

and then on to Whiteside itself, is best relieved
by frequent halts to consume the outstanding
scenery. Across the valley the Loweswater
Fells, Mellbreak especially prominent, instantly draw the eye, while further left rises dome-
shaped Red Pike and the other summits of the
High Stile ridge. Immediately below, beyond
the gashed slopes of Gasgale Crags, lies the
return route, Gasgale Gill, rising to the
impressive broken slopes of Grasmoor End.
With Whin Ben comes the first appearance of
Whiteside and the ensuing ridge, with Grise-

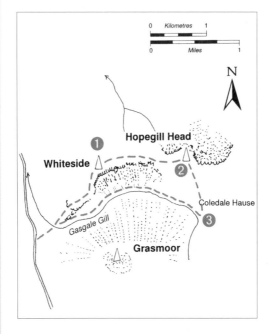

dale Pike peering quizzically through a gap.

As you gain the end of the ridge, do not
assume the nearby cairn (the West Top) marks
the summit of Whiteside (**1**) – that lies a short
distance further on, bypassed by the path and
marked by a small cairn on the edge of the
abyss of Gasgale Gill. The view from the West
Top, however, is a good one, extending across
the Solway Firth to the hills of Galloway.

The continuation to Hopegill Head offers
no choice of route, simply following the ridge
in splendid fashion and then rising dramatically to reach the summit (**2**). Locally the
summit also takes the name Hobcarton Pike.

In the near distance, Grisedale Pike and its
wall-lined unnamed attendant, send steep
slopes northwards into Hobcarton, drawing
strong walkers just that little bit further, not
unreasonably so on a fine day and adding
about 3km/2miles (150m/490ft) to this walk.

To return to Gasgale Gill, leave Hopegill
Head, starting south-east then south to pass
first over rounded Sand Hill before easing
down on a broad, grassy path to Coledale
Hause (**3**), a prominent crossroads from which
many paths radiate.

Gasgale Gill lies west of north-west, fur-
nished with a good path throughout its length,
flanked by imposingly steep slopes and
through which the infant Liza Beck pokes its
way. The final debouchment from its narrow
confines comes with a sense of relief, bursting
forth on the fertile pastures of Lanthwaite
Green, across which lies the starting point.

GRASMOOR

Few would argue that the Lad Hows ridge, sweeping loftily to the summit plateau of Grasmoor is not the finest way of tackling this mighty guardian of Buttermere. Curving upwards in a lazy sweep, the ridge only begins when Lad Hows itself is reached from the pastures of Cinderdale Common, thereafter making a straightforward and spectacular ascent. From valley level, Lad Hows appears as a quite distinct fell, with no apparent link to the much higher mountain to the north.

Combined here with a circuit that takes in the adjacent fells of Wandope and Whiteless Pike, this ascent of Grasmoor ranks among the finest in the Lake District, and follows good paths throughout. The view from the vast summit plateau, a place that can be confusing in mist, is a landscape of Skiddaw Slates and the Borrowdale volcanic rocks that so typify the Lake District. Once these basic rocks were in place they were sculpted by the glaciers of the Ice Age, though Grasmoor and Mellbreak across the valley would both have offered resistance, losing large chunks of their bulk in the process.

Begin from the parking area below Rannerdale Knotts and set off through a gate, bearing right to a footbridge over Squat Beck. Over the beck go left along a track to a gate/stile past a wall. A short way on, to the right, a path starts to move uphill, climbs a little and then strikes diagonally left through bracken to reach a grassy shoulder overlooking Cinderdale Beck. Another bout of uphill work brings you to the cairn on Lad Hows **(1)**.

Only now does the true shape of the ridge come into perspective, rising through heather, never easing much, but quite straightforward, ascending in a majestic sweep to a modest cairn on the edge of the summit plateau. Not far away lies a large multi-directional shelter that marks the highest point of the fell **(2)**.

The plateau is grassy with patches of bare slate, decorated with numerous cairns of both valid and dubious purpose. Among them a small shelter cairn overlooking Crummock Water proves to be a fine vantage point. Grasmoor might equally claim to be called Wild Boar Fell, for the name derives from grise, meaning a wild boar.

The continuation lies due east, pursuing a line of cairns until a prominent path comes into view, leading directly to the col between Grasmoor and Crag Hill. In all but the driest

Grasmoor and Crummock Water from Red Pike

FACT FILE

Start/Finish Parking space near Rannerdale Knotts, GR 163184
Distance 10km (6¼ miles)
Height gain 890m (2920ft)
Walking time 4-5 hours
Type of walk Largely straightforward on clear paths, but the summit of Grasmoor can be confusing in poor visibility. Some sense of exposure above Addacomb Hole (avoidable) and along Whiteless Edge

The Route in Brief

Start Set off from the parking area below Rannerdale Knotts, along through a gate to footbridge over Squat Beck, go L to gate/stile to a path climbing the hillside. Continue to top of Lad Hows.
1 Continue up ridge to summit plateau, going L to summit shelter.
2 Go E to locate descending path to col (with tarns) and climb half R to reach Wandope.
3 Leave Wandope W, then SW to cairn at start of Whiteless Edge. Follow Edge down to Saddle Gate and climb up to Whiteless Pike.
4 Descend Whiteless Breast to col at the head of Rannerdale.
5 Climb a little to traverse ridge to Rannerdale Knotts.
6 Continue briefly northwards, then descend L, either to road or from saddle follow path right to start.

conditions, two small tarns will be found here. From the col, bear half right to reach the steep edge overlooking Addacomb Hole. The contrast between the springy turf slopes leading up to the edge and those that lie beyond could

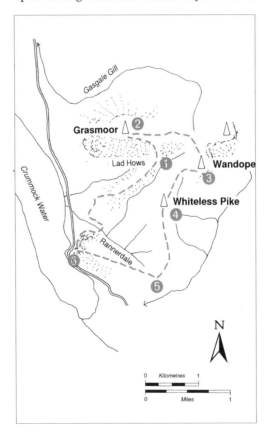

not be greater and may intimidate anyone who suffers from vertigo. From here, should you wish, you can speedily reach the top of Crag Hill, though this approach is far less impressive than that used on the Coledale Horseshoe (Walk 8).

By following the rim above Addacomb Hole you soon reach Wandope (**3**), marked by a cairn. Another cairn, to the west and then south-west, near the head of Third Gill, is reached by an easy descent and marks the start of Whiteless Edge. Be sure, however, to avoid the deceiving start of Wandope's south-west ridge; go west first, until you can clearly see the cairn at the top of the Edge.

Whiteless Edge is a narrow and exhilarating ridge with some sensation of exposure, that plunges down to Saddle Gate before an abrupt haul up again to the top of Whiteless Pike (**4**). Beyond, the path now descends steeply to Whiteless Breast and continues just as steeply to the col above Rannerdale (**5**).

From the col the speedy way down is to drop into the secret valley of Rannerdale, but by climbing a little you move on to the long Rannerdale ridge, passing first over Low Bank before reaching a higher top, Rannerdale Knotts (**6**). The final downward flourish continues north for a short distance before being diverted left by steep crags to reach the road near Hause Point, from where the starting place is easily reached. An alternative line runs right, from a small saddle on this line of descent, directly back to the start.

THE BUTTERMERE HORSESHOE

The basis of this high level walk is simple: beginning from the village of Buttermere, it keeps as much as possible to the watershed of the Buttermere valley, above and around the numerous streams that feed into its lake, no more, no less. *En route* it takes in ten fine fell summits and involves a considerable amount of ascent and descent. This is not a walk for idle curiosity! It is a tough and demanding round, suitable only for fit and experienced mountain walkers. As ever, effort and reward are worthy travelling companions from whom much satisfaction is gained.

The route is not the easiest to follow in poor visibility, and a clear day, with an early morning start, is recommended.

From the village of Buttermere, climb the road past the church and follow it to a lay-by on the right. From here a grassy path (signposted) leaves the road and heads for Robinson, at this point largely unseen. Always climbing, the path crosses the top of a gully and continues in zigzags as it rises to the first objective, a minor top but a wonderful viewpoint, High Snockrigg. Thus far the route has

Fleetwith Pike and the Dubs Quarry

55

Fleetwith Pike and Buttermere

followed the course of an old road used to bring peat down from Buttermere Moss.

It is Buttermere Moss that now faces you beyond High Snockrigg and only here that Robinson fully comes into view. The Moss is a marshy expanse across which the best going tends to be to the right. Once across its clutches, a cairned track rises to a much grander cairn on the edge of Robinson's summit plateau. The main summit (1) lies a short distance away across stony and largely featureless terrain, between two rocky outcrops.

To continue to Hindscarth, head south from the top of Robinson, descending only slightly at first until you encounter a large cairn near a fenceline. Go left here, descending more steeply on a good path to a col at the head of Little Dale, and from there ascend by Littledale Edge to the southern edge of Hindscarth, overlooking Gatesgarthdale. The summit of Hindscarth involves a detour from the watershed in a northerly direction following a cairned path. The highest point is marked by a modest cairn in the centre of another stony plateau.

Returning to the main line, go left (southeast) to pursue Hindscarth Edge directly to the top of Dale Head, which has a splendid outlook across the vale of Newlands and proves to be a superb vantage point in general.

From the top of Dale Head simply head south to Honister Hause (2). This popular mountain road pass is the walk's furthest point east, and, by way of the road descending into the upper Buttermere valley, affords the speediest return to the start if circumstances dictate.

Cross the road, go round the slate works buildings, heading for a conspicuous track climbing the fellside to the west. You ascend by way of an old gravitational railway trackbed which served the quarry industry that flourished here at Honister, notably during the nineteenth century. As the gradient eases so a broad trail appears on the left. Follow this as it heads southwards, rising gently to within a short distance of Grey Knotts.

At any time you can leave it to climb easily over grassy slopes and through low outcrops and boulders to the top of Grey Knotts. A trig pillar marks the highest point, though there is a fine rocky outcrop (cairn) with a good view nearby, of equal height. The top of Grey Knotts is a confusing display of rocky tors and small tarns, from which a line of iron fenceposts runs west of south to Brandreth.

Now, north-west you will see a low outcrop, Great Round How, with Blackbeck Tarn to its left and the knobbly profile of Hay Stacks beyond. If you head towards Great Round How, before reaching it you will intercept the track of the Northern Coast-to-Coast Walk rising from the embrace of Ennerdale and Loft Beck. Beyond the top of Loft Beck a network of vague grassy tracks meander peacefully towards Hay Stacks, a lowly but immensely popular fell top. Or you can divert to reach the main Hay Stacks path near Blackbeck Tarn or Innominate Tarn.

Circumnavigate the tarn on the summit of Hay Stacks (3), and descend rockily to the cairn on Scarth Gap, with, potentially, the most trying section of the walk, Gamlin End, now towering above you. Scarth Gap marks another escape route down to Gatesgarth or along the Buttermere lakeshore if needed.

The bald scree slope of Gamlin End lies near the top of High Crag and is reached by first following a rock and scree path around a minor summit, Seat, more or less accompanying an old fenceline, before engaging the grind up Gamlin End. As you rise steadily up this wearying slope you can take comfort from the knowledge that what lies beyond is a ridge of rare quality.

The summit of High Crag (4), when it comes, is marked by a cairn near an old fenceline and this relic will lead you on to the highest fell along the ridge, High Stile, and then on to Red Pike (5). On a clear day it is worth moving towards the edge overlooking Buttermere, a sculpted masterpiece of natural architecture, invigorating, inspiring and definitely a place to dawdle.

Red Pike marks the terminus of this part of the ridge and from it you descend precariously down a red scree slope path until you meet a constructed pathway and steps. These lead down to Bleaberry Tarn and the quickest way back to Buttermere. But to go that way crosses Sourmilk Gill which, arguably, just flows into the eastern tip of Buttermere lake, and so takes you inside the framework of this walk. If

The final stage: descending to Crummock Water

you disagree, and you may, then the route down via Bleaberry Tarn and Burtness Wood is no less a fitting conclusion to the walk. The alternative, a much quieter end, descends into Ling Comb from the col between Red Pike and Dodd. Either way, the little extra effort needed to visit Dodd is a must, for it is an

Start/Finish Buttermere, GR 173169
Distance 22km (13¾ miles)
Height gain 1805m (5920ft)
Walking time 10-12 hours (variable according to fitness)
Type of walk A strenuous and demanding high level mountain walk; not recommended in poor visibility

The Route in Brief

Start Leave Buttermere and walk up past the church to locate a lay-by and grassy track leading over High Snockrigg and up to Robinson.
1 Continue along ridge to Hindscarth and Dale Head, descending to Honister Pass.
2 Climb by old tramway and turn left along broad track to ease on to Grey Knotts and Brandreth, before heading across country to Hay Stacks.
3 Descend to Scarth Gap and climb around Seat and up Gamlin End to High Crag.
4 Follow ridge over High Stile to Red Pike.
5 Descend to include Dodd and then through Ling Comb to Scales Wood and valley route.
6 Return to Buttermere via Scale Bridge.

outstanding viewpoint, not only for the nearby Chapel Crags of High Stile, but across the vale to Grasmoor and Robinson where you began.

From the col two paths descend towards Ling Comb. Take the one on the left (the other wanders off round Dodd) and this will take you down through heather, becoming less distinct (with deeper heather) the lower you go. Between the top of Far and Near Ruddy Becks the path turns to head for a dilapidated wall, beyond which you may go either left or right, following tracks into Scales Wood, with little to choose between them. Both paths bring you down to the main valley route (6) to Scale Force. When you reach it, turn right to Scale Bridge and cross this to gain a broad track returning you to Buttermere village, to welcome and well-deserved, refreshment.

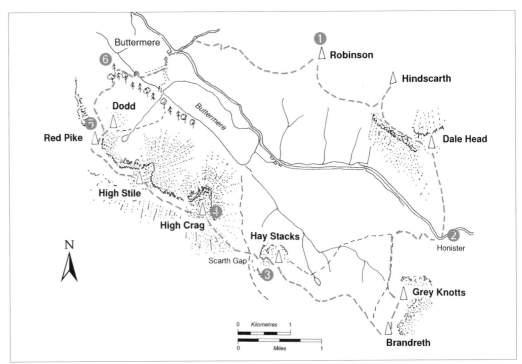

FLEETWITH PIKE AND HAY STACKS

Anyone entering the long valley of Buttermere over the Honister Pass must first pass the stern scrutiny of Fleetwith Pike and its much-quarried sibling, Honister Crag; indeed, from the top of Honister, Fleetwith Pike is easily ascended. Beyond its crag-laden flanks, however, this often-neglected twosome throws down a long, stepped ridge, Fleetwith Edge, to the farm at Gatesgarth, and this makes a most fitting line of ascent, both energetic and breathtaking. As compensation for all the hard work of ascent, this walk continues through the considerably easier, but labyrinthine terrain of heathery knolls and tarns that preludes Hay Stacks, one of the most popular fell tops in Lakeland.

A little to the east of Gatesgarth Farm the path on to Fleetwith Edge leaves the road and begins a steady and unmistakable ascent, every step of which brings improving views of the valley and its flanking fells. A prominent white cross, inscribed 'Erected By Friends of Fanny Mercer Accidentally Killed 1887', provides welcome respite. What the inscription does not tell you is that the accident was as a result of Fanny tripping over the Victorian equivalent of the modern walker's stick. Such fell-poles were regarded as essential walking equipment in Victorian Britain, though they had virtually disappeared from Alpine use by the 1870s.

Beyond the cross, Fleetwith Edge continues its uncompromising rise, bringing you directly to the summit of Fleetwith Pike (1), an outstanding vantage point and a sufficient objective if you began your walk late on a summer's afternoon. It is certainly a wonderful place to watch the sun go down.

The path continues splendidly across the top of Fleetwith Pike to Black Star, the true summit of Honister Crag, only a little lower than Fleetwith Pike, and another good viewpoint. A path through quarry workings leads down from Black Star to reach the old tramway (2) that formerly served the quarries on the fell. When you reach it, turn right and follow its course to the remains of Dubs Quarry.

A short descent leads across Warnscale Beck and on to the rocky lump of Green Crag, from where there is an excellent view down

Tarn on the summit of Hay Stacks

the length of the Buttermere valley. The onward path courses close by the outflow of Blackbeck Tarn, before easing on to the edge of Innominate Tarn, a spot long-favoured by Hay Stacks devotees, but made eternally famous by the wish of Wainwright, former doyen of Lakeland writing, to have his ashes scattered there.

When it comes, the top of Hay Stacks (3) proves to be a refreshing and memorable place, a small tarn below the highest point attracting a disproportionate number of visitors for so (altitudinally) lowly a fell. All around, great fells soar from hidden and tree-cloaked valleys – High Crag, Pillar, Kirk Fell, Great Gable and Green Gable – while the craggy profiles of Brandreth and Grey Knotts dominate the eastern skyline. You could spend all day lounging around on Hay Stacks, and many have!

Pass round the summit tarn to begin a rocky descent to Scarth Gap, an old packhorse route between Buttermere and Ennerdale. Heading northwards, down and across the slopes of Buttermere Fell that rise to High Crag, the old route provides a rough but clear way down to the valley, and a bridge over Warnscale Beck, that puts you on a broad track leading back to Gatesgarth Farm.

Left: Looking down on Buttermere from Hay Stacks

FACT FILE

Start/Finish Car park, Gatesgarth Farm, GR 195150. (Fee payable at the farm)
Distance 8km (5 miles)
Height gain 700m (2295ft)
Walking time About 4 hours
Type of walk A strenuous start leads to much easier going on good, but undulating paths

The Route in Brief

Start Set off from Gatesgarth along the road heading for Honister and soon leave it for a track climbing towards a conspicuous white cross on Fleetwith Edge. Follow the path to the summit.
1 Continue along the top of Fleetwith Pike to Black Star and descend tracks to disused tramway.
2 Go R, past Dubs Quarry (ruins), Blackbeck Tarn and Innominate Tarn to reach summit of Hay Stacks.
3 Descend to Scarth Gap and head N, descending to Warnscale Beck, crossed by a bridge, and follow track out back to start.

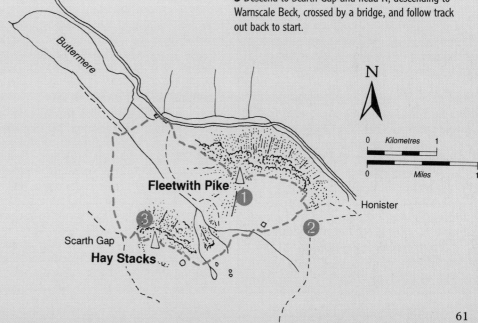

AROUND BUTTERMERE

There is a point, not far from Blackbeck Tarn on the walk to Hay Stacks from Honister, when the ground suddenly drops away from you in a most dramatic fashion to reveal, seemingly far below, the tight length of the Buttermere valley. It is like looking down on some make-believe world, the crag-sided gouge and green flats of Warnscale Bottom leading the eye first to Buttermere and then to Crummock Water beyond. This is the finest way to see Buttermere for the first time, veiled lightly in an early morning mist, when the once oak-wooded slopes, now bare rock, grass and bracken, yield their grandeur but slowly to the vaporising sun.

For a closer acquaintance there is no better appraisal than that which accompanies a tour of the lake itself, a simple affair and suitable for all seasons. The village of Buttermere, its car parks, inns and refreshment, makes the most convenient starting point, though it works no less well from the dale head farm at Gatesgarth.

Begin from the Fish Hotel, renowned in Lakeland lore as the home of Mary Robinson, the so-called Maid (or Beauty) of Buttermere, brought by Captain Budworth to the attention of, among others, the Honourable Alexander Augustus Hope, Lieutenant Colonel in the 14th Regiment of Foot, who wooed and won her, and married her in Lorton church on 2nd October 1802. Alas, Hope was far from honourable, and in fact an imposter, John Hatfield, still with another wife and children from previous marriages. He was eventually hanged, not for bigamy but for forgery in Carlisle in September 1803. Mary married a man from Caldbeck and lived into old age.

Go to the left of the Fish and follow a broad track through gates (ignore the deviation to Scale Force), until, not far from the water's edge, you can turn right along a hedgerow leading to a bridge spanning Buttermere Dubs **(1)**. There is a particularly fine view from this point, along the length of the lake to the sharp profile of Fleetwith Pike at the head of the dale.

Cross the bridge and a small footbridge nearby and go through a gate in a wall at the base of Burtness Wood. Through the gate turn left on a forest track that parallels the

shore of the lake and finally emerges from Burtness Wood not far from Horse Close, where a bridge spans Comb Beck (2). Keep on along the path until you reach a wall leading to a sheepfold and a gate. Go left through the gate, cross Warnscale Beck and press on by a fenced track to Gatesgarth Farm. At the farm take the gate marked 'Lakeside Path', and follow signs to reach the valley road (3).

About 500m/yd of road walking, left, now follows, calling for care in the absence of pathways. As the road bends right, leave it for a footpath on the left (signposted Buttermere via Lakeshore Path). The path shadows a line of holly trees, and leads to a step stile into an open field. Onward the path is never far from the shoreline and brings you to a stand of Scots pine, near Crag Wood, beside which seats and a fine view across the lake raise the temptation to halt for a while.

Beyond Hassnesshow Beck, the trail enters the wooded grounds of Hassness, where a rocky path, enclosed by trees, leads you to a kissing gate. Here a path has been cut into the crag where it plunges into the lake below. Ahead the path disappears into a tunnel, cut by employees of George Benson, a nineteenth-century Manchester mill owner who then owned the Hassness Estate, so that their employer could effect a safe tour of the lake without straying too far from its shore. During

Right: The head of Buttermere

Start/Finish Buttermere village, GR 173169
Distance 7km (4½ miles)
Height gain 40m (130ft)
Walking time 2-2½ hours
Type of walk Easy, on well-maintained paths and tracks; a little road walking

The Route in Brief

Start Leave Buttermere down a track to the left of the Fish Hotel, and continue to reach the lake.

1 Cross a bridge and go through a gate/wall, turning L on forest trail, emerging near Horse Close.

2 Continue to sheepfold and gate, cross Warnscale Beck and walk up to Gatesgarth Farm.

3 Turn L along road to bend and leave it for signposted lakeshore path, through Hassness Estate and tunnel, finally to return via Wilkinsyke Farm to road into Buttermere.

1995 part of the tunnel roof collapsed and the tunnel closed. A signposted diversion will remain in place until the tunnel is made safe.

Beyond the tunnel a gate gives on to a gravel path and a woodland pasture, beyond which you can turn right on a fenced path that crosses a traditional Lakeland bridge of slate slabs. A short way on, through another gate, a path leads you on to Wilkinsyke Farm and an easy walk out to the road, just a short way above the Bridge Hotel in the village.

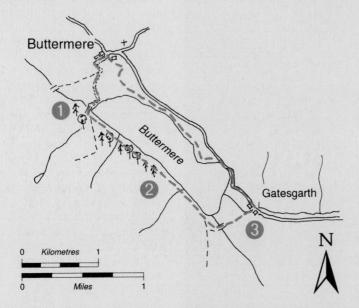

HIGH STILE RIDGE

The trinity of summits that combine to form the High Stile ridge are an inspiring challenge and one that is regularly accepted. Rising in spectacular fashion above the lake of Buttermere, what the ridge lacks in length, it makes up for in natural architecture. It is a long, dark, craggy wall, formed by volcanoes, but from which long-retreated glaciers have gouged the great scoops of Burtness Comb and Bleaberry Comb, the latter containing a fine tarn beside which to rest before the assault on the scree slopes of Red Pike. By contrast the southern aspect, though steep-sided, has been rather less aggravated by glacial action and presents a more rounded posterior to the crags of Pillar and Great Gable.

This walk, which begins with the ascent of Red Pike, ends with a pleasant and easy stroll back beside the lake.

The day begins down an enclosed track to the left of the Fish Hotel in Buttermere that leads to the lake (ignore the turning for Scale Force) and runs down to the foot of Sourmilk Gill which will be found to issue from Bleaberry Tarn high above. Bridges and a gate

The dark crags of High Stile from Dodd

Bleaberry Tarn with the snow-capped Grasmoor group behind

bring you into the bottom of Burtness Wood, with the path that circles the lake going off to the left, while that awaiting your attention strikes a steep diagonal constructed way up through the trees, emerging near a fence, with suitable boulders nearby on which to recover. There is a predictably fine view across the valley to High Snockrigg and Robinson, up-valley to the shapely Fleetwith Pike and northwards to the massive bulk of Grasmoor and its attendants.

Cross the upper boundary fence of Burtness Wood and pursue a reconstructed path rising in energetic fashion to a grassy shelf that brings you back to Sourmilk Gill. Keep the gill on your right and follow obvious pathways through rock, grass and heather, more or less parallel with a wall, until you reach Bleaberry Tarn (1), magnificently set against the bristling face of Chapel Crags. A rounded shelf above the tarn looks as though it ought to contain a smaller lake, but if it ever did, it is long gone.

Although the craggy face of High Stile leans oppressively on Bleaberry Tarn, it is the cone of Red Pike that commands most attention, drawing you to the constructed pathway that rises as far as the col with Dodd, a small outlier of Red Pike, and a worthy diversion.

Beyond the col, the path continues in less accommodating fashion, being well-worn and shaly in places, and potentially intimidating in high winds or icy conditions. Certainly in winter conditions an ice axe is essential here and crampons more than likely useful, too. The same is going to be true for the other end of the ridge, when you descend Gamlin End.

The summit cairn finally appears quite suddenly, a few weary strides from the top of the ascending path (2). A handful of people stride bravely on but most make time for the excellent views not only inward to the far-sprawling fells of Lakeland, but out to the Isle of Man and the Galloway Hills of southern Scotland.

From Red Pike start off south and then south-east, following the rim of the corrie housing Bleaberry Tarn. In poor visibility a line of rusted fenceposts acts as a guide, but in good conditions you can lope along the top of Chapel Crags and on to the rough ground rising to High Stile.

The fenceline that serves to guide walkers on to High Stile continues its duties on to High Crag, though here too on a clear day you can wander above the crags of Burtness Comb. These crags are steeper than Chapel Crags and beneath winter snow especially could be a trap for the unwary. The top of High Crag is also marked by a prominent cairn.

Now all that remains is to descend to Scarth Gap, down the loose scree slopes of Gamlin End, where caution is very much the watchword. Once the lower section is reached the path passes by a minor summit, Seat, before heading down to the cairn on Scarth Gap (3). A left turn here will take you down the rocky road to the valley, and a fine walk back along the southern shore of Buttermere and through Burtness Wood to rejoin your outward route near Sourmilk Gill.

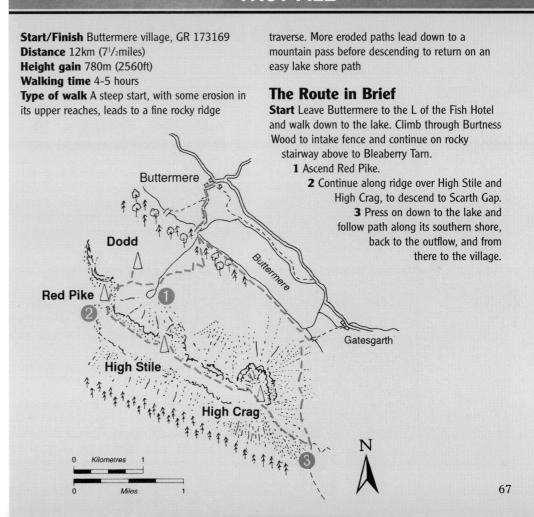

FACT FILE

Start/Finish Buttermere village, GR 173169
Distance 12km (7½miles)
Height gain 780m (2560ft)
Walking time 4-5 hours
Type of walk A steep start, with some erosion in its upper reaches, leads to a fine rocky ridge traverse. More eroded paths lead down to a mountain pass before descending to return on an easy lake shore path

The Route in Brief

Start Leave Buttermere to the L of the Fish Hotel and walk down to the lake. Climb through Burtness Wood to intake fence and continue on rocky stairway above to Bleaberry Tarn.

1 Ascend Red Pike.

2 Continue along ridge over High Stile and High Crag, to descend to Scarth Gap.

3 Press on down to the lake and follow path along its southern shore, back to the outflow, and from there to the village.

Buttermere

Dodd

Red Pike

Buttermere

Gatesgarth

High Stile

High Crag

N

0   Kilometres   1

0   Miles   1

RED PIKE TO GREAT BORNE
AND SCALE FORCE

It is difficult to imagine anyone labouring up the loose scree slopes of Red Pike from Buttermere only, on reaching the summit, to shun the obvious craggy attractions of High Stile to the south-east for the grassy promenade across Starling Dodd and Great Borne. Indeed, few walkers take these westering steps, which is all to the good if you enjoy comparative solitude and easy walking, and they bear an agreeable charm that makes this walk a fine alternative to more popular routes, especially in summer.

Once the spreading expanse of these turfy fells is crossed, the walk wends a wonderful way back to Buttermere by Floutern Tarn and the southern flanks of the Loweswater Fells before visiting Scale Force, objective of many a Victorian excursion.

The route to Red Pike is adequately described in Walk 17 and need not be repeated here, except to remind about the eroded nature of the final section of the ascent to the top of Red Pike. It can be a little intimidating,

especially in windy conditions. In winter, an ice axe and possibly crampons may prove necessary.

From the superb vantage point of Red Pike (1) summit start off north-west, following an intermittent line of cairns before descending to intercept an old fenceline. On a clear day you can make directly for Starling Dodd (2), either directly over or flanking the minor lump, Little Dodd. The top of Starling Dodd is a bare dome of grass peppered with small rocks and adorned by a bizarre cairn sprouting an array of tangled metal posts that were once the stanchions of a former fence. From the top of Starling Dodd there is a good view up the length of Ennerdale, to Pillar, Kirk Fell, Great Gable and Green Gable.

Beyond Starling Dodd rises the grey, rocky bulk of Great Borne. This is easily and leisurely reached on a clear path that eventually runs parallel with a fenceline ascending to the summit. A convenient stile tempts you into

Left: Red Pike (Buttermere)
Right: Starling Dodd and Great Borne from the summit of Red Pike

FACT FILE

Start/Finish Buttermere village, GR 173169
Distance 14km (8¾ miles)
Height gain 860m (2820ft)
Walking time 4-5 hours
Type of walk A steep start through woods and up scree slopes leads to a fine, elevated walk mostly on grass and clear paths. Another steep descent into boggy terrain precedes a fine walk out to the finish

The Route in Brief

Start Leave Buttermere past the Fish Hotel and follow track to lake, from there ascending through Burtness Wood to Red Pike.

1 Descend NW to intercept old fenceline and follow this over Little Dodd and Starling Dodd.
2 Continue along fenceline to Great Borne.
3 Descend steeply to top of Floutern Pass, and turn R.
4 Drop easily into the head of Mosedale (past Floutern Tarn), and keep on to Scale Force.
5 Cross bridge at foot of Scale Force, and follow path round to Scale Bridge, crossing to return by enclosed track to Buttermere.

crossing the fence but there is no need, for the highest point of the fell, marked by a trig pillar **(3)**, lies on the south side of the fence.

After Great Borne you set off in a north-westerly direction turning to northerly as you descend very steeply to the boggy Floutern Pass **(4)**. From here to Scale Force it is unusual to encounter other walkers. A path moves down towards the wide and very boggy clutch of Mosedale, though much can be avoided. First, however, comes Floutern Tarn (flow-tarn, the tarn of the bog), housed, unseen, in a dip. Further on, beyond a couple of fences and stiles, you have to mix it with some wet patches as you move across the mouth of Mosedale, because there is no clear cut, and certainly no dry, line to take. If you aim half right, trending towards the steepness of Gale Fell, you are eventually united with a much-improved path that will take you past Scale Force. In some years the way across this hiatus is self-evident, in others it is not and much depends on the rainfall.

Scale Force **(5)** marks a suitable place for a final halt before following the clear path round to the sparseness of Scales Wood and Scale Bridge, from where a broad track will lead you back to Buttermere village.

AROUND CRUMMOCK WATER

In company with neighbouring Buttermere and Loweswater, Crummock Water once formed a single massive glacial lake only to become forcibly separated by debris brought down from the high fells that frame both the valley of Buttermere and the equally delectable Vale of Lorton. The lake is one of Lakeland's deepest, once famous for its char, which in the seventeenth and eighteenth centuries found their way into such Lakeland delicacies as potted char and char pie. The name 'crummock' derives from the Gaelic, *cromach*, a crook, thought to refer to the forced hooking of the lake around the awkwardness of Hause Point.

The complete circuit of Crummock Water is a splendid valley walk suitable for any time of year though prone to bogginess in places. The opportunity is taken to visit one of Lakeland's most popular Victorian attractions, Scale Force.

The walk may be undertaken either from Buttermere, or, as here, from the northern and rather quieter end of the lake, at Scale Hill. Buttermere village therefore becomes an ideal and logical place to halt for lunch.

From the car park at Scale Hill take the broad path into Lanthwaite Wood. Once through a gate continue to a forked junction and go right to reach the lake shore (1). When you arrive at the lake, cross the outlet by footbridges and join a path down the western shoreline. Beyond in-flowing Park Beck, the path is joined by another, near evidence of earthworks, marked as 'Peel' on the map, suggesting that there would have been a pele tower here in times gone by, no doubt as fortification against reivers during Border troubles, notably during the sixteenth century.

With the enormous bulk of Grasmoor as a constant attendant across the lake, the path continues at two levels to reach the finger-like protuberance of Low Ling Crag, which used to be the landing stage for the boats of visiting Victorians bound for Scale Force.

Just inland from Low Ling Crag is the rock outcrop of High Ling Crag and beyond this the path moves away from the lake on a rough track alongside Scale Beck to a footbridge spanning Black Beck, above which another footbridge is met at the very foot of Scale Force (2). Exploration of the falls is rarely a totally dry experience, its dank chasm formed by water debouching from the moors above at a point where hard granophyre meets the easily-eroded Skiddaw slates.

Across the base footbridge, a good path now leads on below Blea Crag and the slopes of Ling Comb into Scales Wood, crossing Buttermere Dubs at Scale Bridge. Beyond this fine bridge a broad track leads up to Buttermere village (3) and a timely break.

Leaving Buttermere involves a short stretch of road walking. Go left at the Bridge Hotel, over Mill Beck and along the road until, just as it approaches the shoreline, you can leave it on the right for an easily ascending green track that climbs behind Hause Point, descending in zigzags to the road once more, near a car park. Walk through the car park and, keeping to the left wall, soon reach a gate beyond which the remains of a stone wall steer you to a bridge spanning Rannerdale Beck.

Once over the beck, go left, continuing across Cinderdale Common (4), so named from the cindered remains of the smelting that once went on in this area. The way brings you via cross-flowing Cinderdale Beck, back to the road again, followed northwards for a short distance, before leaving it on the left at a gate. Steps take you down to the lakeshore and along a path into High Wood and to the boathouse on the lake shore. Beyond the boathouse re-enter Lanthwaite Wood, soon reaching the path used on the outward journey.

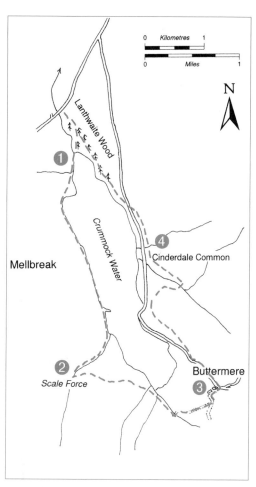

Mellbreak and Crummock Water

FACT FILE

Start/Finish Scalehill Bridge car park, GR 149215
Distance 14.5km (9 miles)
Height gain 240m (785ft)
Walking time Allow 5+ hours
Type of walk Mixed walking, boggy in a few places. Farm and forest tracks, green trails and stony fellside paths, and a few unbridged streams that could be difficult after prolonged wet weather

The Route in Brief

Start Leave the car park and head into Lanthwaite Wood, continuing to the lakeshore, crossing by footbridges to a path on the western shore.
1 Follow path to Low Ling Crag, and up to Scale Force.
2 Keep with path beyond Scale Force, crossing Buttermere Dubs by Scale Bridge, and up to village.
3 Turn L up valley road until reaching a grassy track climbing behind Hause Point. Descend to car park, and follow track round to Cinderdale Common.
4 Along road to gate on L, descending to shoreline, and continuing through woodland to return to start.

GREAT GABLE

It may seem an arrogance to embrace a group of fine and, in many ways, independent, mountains under the umbrella of just one of their number, but Great Gable is universally held in high esteem and its greater glory reflects strongly on the surrounding fells of its company. Yet you cannot escape the fact that anyone walking within the Gables group is invariably heading for Great Gable, incidental to which might be the ascent of an adjoining peak.

As Walt Unsworth, President of the Outdoor Writers' Guild reminds us, 'Great Gable represents the spirit of Lakeland. It is the quintessential fell; the one remembered when others are forgotten. Gable is as much romance as reality, like the Matterhorn, and just as the Matterhorn symbolizes the Alps so too Gable symbolizes Lakeland'.

The summit of Great Gable is owned by the National Trust, given in 1923 by the Fell and Rock Climbing Club as a memorial to its members killed in the First World War. Each year a service of remembrance is held on the summit.

Great Gable from the Corridor Route to Scafell Pike

Certainly Great Gable is regarded with affection both by walkers and rock climbers alike, offering something for everyone. There are excellent routes to its summit, cliff faces to occupy the cragsfolk for many a day, tracks that pass all around it allowing low level perambulations, and ever-present the knowledge that no ascent can be disappointing. And if its very highest point seems a confusing and uninteresting array of boulders, you have only to walk the short distance to the Westmorland Cairn to stand before one of the finest, and for many, *the* finest view to be found in the Lake District.

With Wasdale at your feet, you gaze down on a Promised Land of rolling hills, of acres green set against a great lake and dark walls of fallen rocks.

Beside Great Gable, Kirk Fell, with its double-topped summit and tiny tarns, is comparatively seldom visited, unhappily sandwiched between two of Lakeland's major fells. Yet it provides a welcome change on crowded days. Green Gable, joined tenuously to Great Gable by Windy Gap, on the other hand is frequently passed over by walkers bound for Great Gable. But time should be allowed to absorb its fine situation at the head of Ennerdale and Gillercomb and its marvellous views not only of Great Gable itself, but of Great End, Sty Head and Glaramara.

Evidence suggests that Windy Gap was a gateway used by prehistoric man as he commuted from the axe factories on the Langdale Pikes to the coastal plains. Either side of Windy Gap untidy scree runnels lead speedily down to Sty Head or the upper reaches of Ennerdale, making this a logical and obvious crossing point. Aaron Slack, once known as Erne Slack, leads from Sty Head across to Stone Cove, a description that says it all.

From Green Gable a rough ridge runs northwards, over Brandreth and Grey Knotts to Honister and Fleetwith Moss. In days gone by, Honister was a scene of bustling activity as the much-prized Honister Green Slate was eased from the quarries by hard men doing hard work.

With the notable exception of the classic view of Great Gable at the head of Wasdale, however, the entire group is not well seen from a distance. True, Great Gable's conspicuous pate pokes into many panoramas, but for the best imagery you need to be among the folds and gullies, the heathered flanks and soaring buttresses. For then it is that you gain an intimacy, heightened by proximity, that on this occasion distance cannot give.

BASE BROWN AND THE GABLES

Great Gable, icon of the Lake District National Park, ranks among the most popular of the Lakeland summits; indeed, it is a mountain so intimately known and loved by fell walker and rock climber alike that the millions of feet to which it has been subjected have finally trampled it close to death. Yet it remains a great mountain with great charm, and few are the mountain-top panoramas of Lakeland that do not feature Gable's rounded pate somewhere in the scene.

Immediately adjacent, Green Gable, an equally fine mountain, suffers from the proximity of its mighty neighbour and is largely used as a stepping stone. Few, if any, walkers reaching the top of Green Gable decline the final plunge across Windy Gap and the rocky scramble to the top of Great Gable. The first objective on this walk, however, is Base Brown, a logical extension of both Gables but one that really is often neglected.

The day begins from Seatoller, rather than Seathwaite, starting and finishing along a stretch of the Allerdale Ramble, which can be omitted. But this modest addition will tax no one: it simply prolongs an eminently enjoyable walk.

Leave the car park at Seatoller and turn left down the road, following it round (towards Rosthwaite) until you cross the River Derwent at Strands Bridge. Go immediately right after the bridge on a broad track (signposted Seathwaite) that services Thornythwaite Farm, but keep on when the track heads for the farm, sticking to a pleasant path that soon joins Black Sike and wanders on to Seathwaite (1) amid farmland pastures.

Go between the buildings at Seathwaite and leave through arch signposted to the camp site. Continue to a bridge spanning the Derwent and keep ahead to court the cascade of Sourmilk Gill, spilling from the hanging valley of Gillercomb above. Beyond a wall a path goes behind Seathwaite Slabs, an easy-angled rock playground for novices. As the path zigzags so it provides a fine view of the topmost fall before the gradient eases.

At the top of Sourmilk Gill you cross a morainic ridge formed when the corrie glacier that gouged out Gillercomb finally lost its impetus and deposited its burden of debris. This high, hidden valley evades casual observation but provides a natural approach to the Gables.

Across the comb, Raven Crag is a popular cliff with rock climbers, while Base Brown rears massively above you on the left. A good path continues into Gillercomb, but this is abandoned when a balanced boulder appears on the skyline to the left. Climb diagonally and steeply towards it and go left beneath the crag, named Hanging Stone. It looks worse than it is and has little or no path to begin with, but when one does appear, it leads you easily upwards to the summit of Base Brown (2), marked by a cairn.

Continue in a south-westerly direction to cross the easy col before Green Gable, where the path from Gillercomb arrives. Follow this to the stony top of Green Gable (3), descend a scree path to cross Windy Gap (with an escape left down Aaron Slack), and climb the rock and scree that leads you to the splendid summit plateau of Great Gable (4).

From the Westmorland Cairn, erected by the Westmorland brothers in 1876 on the southern edge of the plateau, there is the finest mountain landscape in this part of Lakeland, a contention that would raise little dissent.

Return to the main cairn and pursue a well-trodden path descending the Breast Route (repaired in recent times) to Sty Head (5).

Great Gable and Green Gable

FACT FILE

Start/Finish Seatoller car park, GR 245138
Distance 14km (8³/₄ miles)
Height gain 885m (2905ft)
Walking time 5 hours
Type of walk A rugged high mountain walk; physically demanding

The Route in Brief

Start From Seatoller car park go L to Strands Bridge, then by farm access and path to Seathwaite. This initial section can be omitted by parking at Seathwaite.
1 Go through arch in building and climb by Sourmilk Gill into Gillercomb. At the entrance to this upper valley, climb steeply L, past Hanging Stone to reach the top of Base Brown.
2 Cross shallow col and ascend to Green Gable.
3 Descend path across Windy Gap, and pursue rocky trail to summit of Great Gable.

4 Descend Breast Route to Sty Head.
5 Go L, past Styhead Tarn and at bridge keep L, to descend by way of Taylorgill Force, returning through farm fields to Seathwaite. Retrace outward steps from Seathwaite, or follow road to Seatoller.

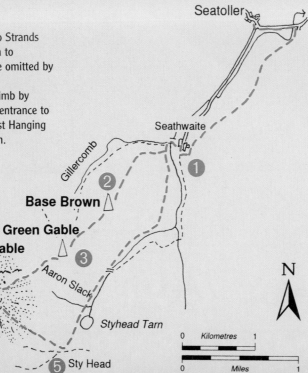

When you reach this mountain crossroads, go left towards Styhead Tarn, passing beneath Aaron Slack, having earlier strolled across its top. At a bridge, keep to the true left bank of Styhead Gill, dropping into the wooded confines of Taylorgill Force, a splendid cataract that is not visible from the conventional route to Sty Head via Stockley Bridge. A little (easy) rock scrambling awaits, as the path crosses a ledge, goes through a gate and continues downwards, soon to reach the open flats that lead northwards back to the Seathwaite bridge over the Derwent.

From Seathwaite either retrace your outward steps to Strands Bridge and Seatoller, or simply stroll along the road, taking care in the absence of a roadside footpath.

THE FOUR PASSES

Suitable even for days when the tops are draped in mist, the Four Passes walk is an utterly refreshing circuit that slips neatly into any serious walker's portfolio. Its basic construction is simple: you link the valleys of Borrowdale, Wasdale, Ennerdale and Buttermere by crossing four passes, Sty Head, Black Sails, Scarth Gap and Honister.

Being circular, and touching base in each valley, you can plug into the circuit anywhere. Since places where refreshments may be obtained are few – Seathwaite, Wasdale Head and, perhaps, Gatesgarth being the exception – and the opportunities to relax and enjoy the views many, it is wise to go well-provisioned. This is a walk to be savoured, and like any feast it will be enjoyed all the better for a leisurely approach, especially in summer, resting, eating and drinking frequently.

The following description begins at Seatoller in Borrowdale, where there is a convenient car park and toilets, and favours a clockwise direction.

Approaching Sty Head

The walk begins innocuously enough, ambling down the road from Seatoller to Seathwaite (1); a gentle introduction to warm up limbs. Beyond the farm buildings a broad path continues to escort the combined forces of Styhead Gill and Grains Gill, here the River Derwent, as far as the old packhorse bridge, Stockley Bridge (2). Through a gate, ignoring a track going left beside a wall, a path ahead injects a little ascent, pulling up towards a small plantation that conceals the white mare's tail of Taylorgill Force. Climbing steadily, a rough track presses on to a wooden bridge spanning Styhead Gill, beyond which Styhead Tarn reposes in a vast hollow flanked by some of the highest of Lakeland's mountains – Great Gable, Lingmell, Scafell Pike, Broad Crag, Great End.

Between Seathwaite and the wooden bridge spanning Styhead Gill, a variant route with a better view of Taylorgill Force is available. This leaves Seathwaite by an archway through barns, as if heading for Sourmilk Gill and the hanging valley of Gillercombe. Once the Derwent is crossed, however, a path, initially muddy, skirts the bottom of a small copse, roughly parallel with the Stockley Bridge path. Gradually this climbs and later turns the corner of Base Brown and scampers to a gate in a most curious spot. A little nimble footwork on easy rising rocks soon leads on towards Taylorgill Force, followed by a steady rise, keeping close by Styhead Gill, to the wooden bridge and before long Sty Head Pass.

Sty Head (3) is unquestionably one of the finest spots in Lakeland and a popular crossroads as walkers launch themselves in all directions. Not surprisingly a number of tracks radiate from Sty Head and a little caution is needed to get the right one, heading down towards Wasdale, high above Lingmell Beck. The valley bottom is reached near Burnthwaite Farm, one of only a few farms remaining active in Wasdale.

Mosedale awaits, and at its head, the great bulk of Pillar, an inevitable attraction for anyone based in Wasdale and Ennerdale. Both these valleys have long been popular with walkers, though their relative inaccessibility tends to keep out the idly curious.

Into Mosedale an easy path leads on, trekking round the base of Kirk Fell before rising a little more sternly by Gatherstone Beck to Black Sail Pass (4). Anyone suddenly finding themselves needing to return to Seatoller can use an undulating trod crossing from just below the Black Sail Pass to Beck Head, between Great Gable and Kirk Fell (East Top), and from there following Moses' Trod to Honister. Moses is said to have been an illicit whisky distiller, working furtively on the slopes of Fleetwith Pike; more likely he was helping himself to plumbago, which in those days brought a good price especially on the black market.

Onward the route descends sharply to the head of Ennerdale, arriving without complication at Black Sail Youth Hostel (5), one of the most imaginatively sited youth hostels in England and an ideal base for anyone wanting to tackle this walk or the ascent of surrounding peaks over a few days.

Traffic is prohibited in Ennerdale and results in the preservation here of a wild and rugged landscape. The once serried ranks of conifer that flanked the valley have seen some realignment, felling and replanting in recent years that has eased much of Ennerdale Forest's former rigidity, making it altogether a better place to wander.

Beyond the youth hostel, the walk keeps to the northern edge of the forest, rising easily to Scarth Gap (6), with the great scree slope of Gamlin End rising to High Crag on the one hand and less demanding Hay Stacks on the other. From here a path descending to Gatesgarth Farm at the head of the Buttermere valley is pursued, there heading east, up the B5289 for the top of Honister.

Such, at least, is the conventional route, but walking up a road pass is unlikely to appeal to many when a vastly superior alternative is to hand.

From Scarth Gap a variant finish to this particular sequence of passes heads up the rock shoulder of Hay Stacks and from there out across the great plateau of knolls and hollows between Hay Stacks and Honister. Innominate Tarn is first reached, a place of some poignancy for walkers reared on the lakeland gospels according to the late Alfred Wainwright, for here, in accordance with his wishes, his ashes

were scattered so that he might finally rest in a place he loved with a great passion.

Blackbeck Tarn, a little further on has rather less appeal, though Nature's architecture here perfectly frames a picture of Buttermere beyond Warnscale Bottom. On crossing Black Beck a path ascends to the remains of Dubs Quarry, where a few ruinous buildings mark the start of a long gradual climb to a point overlooking the slate quarry at Honister **(7)**.

A short way down the road from Honister Hause a track branches left. This was the original line down to Borrowdale and a toll road

Along the Four Passes: High Crag and Hay Stacks

that now sees a steady flow of pedestrian traffic. As Seatoller is reached, the old road swings round to meet the new road at a gate near a national park information centre, followed by a short stroll back to the starting point.

Start/Finish Car park, Seatoller, GR 245138
Distance 22km (13³/₄miles) – 2.5km (1¹/₂miles)
less via Hay Stacks
Height gain Full circuit 1195m (3920ft)
Via Hay Stacks 1105m (3625ft)
Walking time 6-7 hours
Type of walk Long and energetic mountain
walk; good tracks throughout

The Route in Brief

Start Start at Seatoller and walk down the road to
Seathwaite.
1 Follow track to Stockley Bridge.
2 Ascend to Sty Head.
3 Descend into Wasdale and turn R into Mosedale,
climbing to Black Sail Pass.
4 Descend to Black Sail Youth Hostel.
5 Climb to Scarth Gap. Variant: Ascend Hay Stacks
and cross undulating terrain to Honister direct.
6 Descend to Buttermere (Gatesgarth), and ascend
road to Honister Pass.
7 Descend from Honister on road and track to
Seatoller.

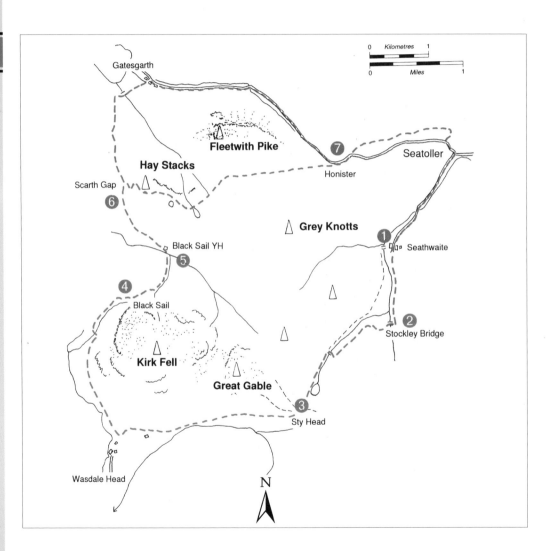

GREAT GABLE VIA NAPES NEEDLE

Walkers tackling the Scottish Munros sooner or later have to face the Inaccessible Pinnacle on Skye. In North Wales, less daunting but no less impressive, Bristly Ridge or Crib Goch require the hands-on approach of those who seek out the best. In the Lake District you 'Thread the Needle' by passing behind (not over, thankfully) Napes Needle on the massive southern face of Great Gable.

Though all of these are outstanding routes, some would argue (with justification) that there is much worse. Yet they have in common a threshold that for many walkers is a psychological barrier. Napes Needle, let it be said, while no less worthy of the company of the others, is a problem that can be surmounted with only a modest degree of ungainly effort – my glasses fell off when I first thrutched up it. Accomplish the 'Needle' and your reward is one of the most outstanding viewpoints in the Lake District, so do remember to take your camera!

This walk begins at Seathwaite and rises to Sty Head, but you can tackle the route to Sty Head just as easily from Wasdale.

Great Gable, showing the conspicuous screes of Great Hell Gate

83

Napes Needle

From Seathwaite two routes approach Sty Head. One goes through the arch in the farm buildings, crosses the River Derwent by a footbridge and then turns immediately left to follow a path running along below Base Brown to climb by Taylorgill Force. The other stays in the valley bottom as far as Stockley Bridge and ascends from there across the northern slopes of Seathwaite Fell. The latter, though longer, is less rugged underfoot and tends to be quicker. Both paths join at a footbridge over Styhead Gill and continue easily to Sty Head (1).

What follows now requires good walking fitness and modest scrambling ability, though the scrambling can all be avoided. Because the Napes lie high on the southern slope of Great Gable, they convey a mild sense of exposure, but this should deter no one.

From Sty Head a path slopes across the fellside between the Breast Route up Great Gable and the way down to Wasdale. In a short time you reach the first major rock feature, Kern Knotts, a massive downfall of boulders spreading below its face. Two immense cracks split the face. That on the right, Innominate Crack, is the more difficult and was unclimbed until 1922. On the left, Kern Knotts Crack was first ascended by Owen Glynne Jones in 1897.

The onward path, known as the South Traverse, forms part of a complete girdle of Great Gable and it continues now below Kern Knotts, clear but occasionally narrow and increasingly higher above the valley below. As you round a corner so the Napes spring into view, a sensational thrust of outcrops and rocky ridges projecting from the scree-laden slopes of the mountain.

The first obstacle of note is Great Hell Gate (2), a massive runnel of red screes and boulders, which is soon crossed. As the rocky ridges of the Napes and the Needle become more defined, so the path splits. The lower, left, path skips the visit to the Needle, and continues to the next scree runnel, Little Hell Gate. The higher path leads to a point directly below the Needle. From here walkers with some scrambling ability should ascend directly to the Needle, but keeping slightly to the right of it, climbing by a narrow gully with polished, but ample, holds. At the top of the gully, with towering cliffs on your right and the reverse side of the Needle to your left, you finally 'Thread the Needle' and cross a narrow rock threshold to descend a little awkwardly into Needle Gully. A quick stride across the gully brings you to the base of Abbey Buttress and a comfortable rock platform known as the Dress Circle (3), since from it you can spend hours watching the antics of rock climbers on the Needle.

The Needle was first climbed solo in 1886, by Walter Parry Haskett-Smith, a barrister and philologist, in a bold ascent commonly regarded as the birth of rock climbing as an individual sport.

A short distance beyond the Dress Circle, across an awkward little slab with more polished holds, an upthrust of rock provides another resting place from which to look forward to Arrowhead Gully and its own rock feature, Sphinx Rock.

Viewed from below, Sphinx Rock resembles a cat and is as a result also known as Cat Rock. The classic 'sphinx-like' profile, however, looks more like an American Indian chief with the tip of his feather broken off!

The South Traverse passes beneath Sphinx Rock to reach Little Hell Gate around a corner. The route now lies upwards, following an indistinct path very steeply up the right side of the scree to the top of the Napes Ridges. Here, seemingly barring further progress, you face Westmorland Crags, which guard the top of the mountain. These, fortunately, are easily turned on the left, on a track that leads you to the Westmorland Cairn and a marvellous retrospective view of Wasdale. The highest point of Great Gable (4) lies a short way to the north.

From the summit locate the rocky track going north-east and descending, in the direction of Green Gable, to Windy Gap (5). Windy Gap provides you with a choice: either ascend Green Gable and drop into Gillercomb, to finish the walk beside Sourmilk Gill (the most direct option), or go down Aaron Slack, a broad scree gully that brings you to the main Sty Head path not far from Styhead Tarn. Once on the main path, you simply retrace your steps to Seathwaite.

FACT FILE

Start/Finish Seathwaite, GR 235122
Distance 10km (6¹/₄ miles)
Height gain 770m (2525ft)
Walking time Allow 5+ hours
Type of walk Rough and rocky, but mostly on clear paths. Some rock scrambling (avoidable) and steep scree slopes both to cross and ascend. A strenuous walk

The Route in Brief

Start From Seathwaite follow either of two routes to Sty Head.
1 Locate the South Traverse, between the Breast Route to Great Gable and the descending Wasdale path, and follow this past Kern Knotts and Great Hell Gate.
2 Either continue the South Traverse, or climb to the right of Napes Needle, scrambling behind it and descend into Needle Gully. Cross the gully to reach rocky platform.
3 Continue awkwardly on to rejoin South Traverse, past Sphinx Rock to Little Hell Gate, and turn R, ascending Little Hell Gate (on the R) to Westmorland Crags and the summit of Great Gable.
4 Descend to Windy Gap.
5 Either cross Green Gable and descend through Gillercomb, or descend Aaron Slack to rejoin outward route near Styhead Tarn.

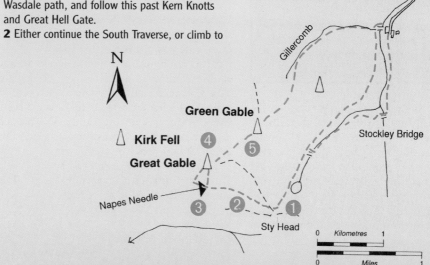

THE GABLES AND KIRK FELL FROM HONISTER

Supposedly named after an illicit whisky distiller, Moses Trod was once a packhorse route linking Honister, Wasdale and beyond. Today it is the key to the easiest ascent of Great Gable, an excursion that can be extended to take in Kirk Fell as well, so enabling a splendid walk throughout which the constant vision of Great Gable and Kirk Fell has a magnetic effect. For much of the way the going underfoot is remarkably easy, and with your objective never out of sight once the initial climb on to Fleetwith Moor has been accomplished, this approach cannot be bettered.

Leave the car park at the rear of the youth hostel by steps next to the slate works. Go left along the road to a gate giving access to the slate works yard. Cross the yard to start up the prominent track, the old tramway down which slate was brought from the quarries, signposted to Great Gable and the Dubs Quarry. A little zigzagging takes some of the sting out of the short-lived ascent and before long the gradient relents as the edge of Fleetwith Moor is reached.

Moses Trod leaves the trackbed and goes left (south), bypassing both Grey Knotts and Brandreth, to which easy deviations can be made. This short stretch now forms part of the Northern Coast-to-Coast Walk, which between Grey Knotts and Brandreth departs for the top of Loft Beck and Ennerdale.

Further on, Moses Trod moves right to pass below Great Gable, making for Beck Head, from where it drops into Wasdale. Keep always to the main track and gradually it will bring you round to Gillercomb Head and up on to Green Gable (1).

All along this section the scenery is superb,

Kirk Fell and Great Gable from Red Pike (Wasdale)

embracing Buttermere, Crummock Water, the High Stile ridge, Ennerdale and Pillar.

From Green Gable you need to descend a scree path to Windy Gap, from where the on-going path to Great Gable (2) climbs steeply and rockily, popping out on to the summit with agreeable suddenness.

Having explored the top of Gable, including a visit to the Westmorland Cairn from which you look down on one of the most memorable landscapes in Lakeland, take care to orientate yourself correctly, north-west, to find a well-trodden path setting off steeply down to Beck Head. This can be confusing in mist, not aided by a few false paths that have evolved. As you descend the ridge, however, you meet a line of fenceposts and these now guide you safely across the high col of Beck Head (turn right for Moses Trod and a speedy return to Honister), and up Rib End on to twin-topped Kirk Fell (3). In clear conditions you can wander about easily on Kirk Fell's rock-punctuated grassy plateau; at other times the fenceposts will be needed for guidance, though they never quite touch upon the two highest points. Between the two summits, two small tarns share the name, Kirkfell Tarn.

The quickest way back is to retreat to Beck Head, but if the day is fine continue again in a north-westerly direction, still roughly following fenceposts, and you will descend very steeply through the broken rocks and scree of Kirkfell Crags to reach the top of Black Sail Pass (4). This can be an awkward descent and

care must be exercised if you want to reach the pass safely.

Just below the pass on the Ennerdale side, a narrow path undulates across the northern slopes of Kirk Fell, finally rising to regain Beck Head (5). As it does so you can continue this time below the northern crags of Great Gable to cross Stony Cove, the northern equivalent of Aaron Slack. The going is quite rocky, though the path can be muddy in places.

Once beyond Greengable Crag and Giller-comb Head you are back on familiar ground, retracing your outward steps to Honister.

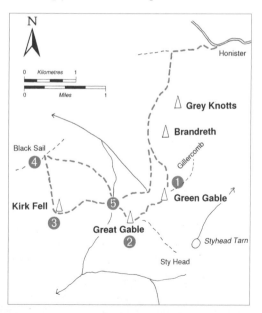

FACT FILE

Start/Finish Honister Pass car park, GR 225135
Distance 13km (8 miles)
Height gain 960m (3150ft)
Walking time 5-6 hours
Type of walk A demanding walk with considerable height gain that traverses three major summits. Suitable for strong walkers only, and not recommended in poor visibility

The Route in Brief

Start Leave Honister car park and climb the track leading up on to Fleetwith Moor. As the gradient levels, go left along Moses Trod, ignoring deviations until you leave it to climb to Green Gable.
1 Cross Windy Gap and climb rockily on to Great Gable.
2 Descend NW ridge to Beck Head (5), and ascend Rib End on to Kirk Fell, following fenceposts.
3 Again descend, with care, NW, through Kirkfell Crags to reach Black Sail Pass.
4 Locate path on N side of pass, undulating across N side of Kirk Fell, and climbing once more to Beck Head.
5 Continue below Great Gable, across Stone Cove and rejoin Moses Trod on the flanks of Brandreth, retracing outward steps to Honister.

5

ENNERDALE AND WASDALE

Ennerdale has been much maligned in recent years as a result of large-scale tree planting that cloaked the fellsides in angular lines of dark green conifers. Today, some of the trees have been felled and a more enlightened view taken of the impact forestry plantations can have on a wild landscape. As a result, the scenery is vastly improved and a few steps taken towards a balanced and sensible compromise. Now, from within the mantle of green, cameos of fellsides, streams and peaks flit softly by, brightening the scene and lightening the step.

Yet few visitors to Ennerdale are able to see the true wilderness that lies at its head, for there is no unauthorised access to the dale by car beyond Bowness Knott. From the shores of the lake, only an impression of what awaits the pedestrian up-dale can be gained, and that a vague one at best. For here rise great crag-girt summits in striking array, an inspiring and moving display amid which the sense of isolation from the outside world is most marked. Those who have sat on the steps of Black Sail Youth Hostel and watched the moon rising

Beside the River Liza (Ennerdale)

over Great Gable and Pillar or the pale last light of day give way to a brightly starred heaven will be closer than most to touching the true spirit of Lakeland.

Beyond the great lake, the River Liza finds its way down from the slopes of Pillar, Kirk Fell, Great Gable, Brandreth and the Buttermere Fells, penetrating the mantle of green darkness in its dash for the embrace of Ennerdale Water. From the head of the dale escape routes to adjoining valleys lie over ancient packhorse trails, via Scarth Gap to Buttermere and Black Sail Pass to the heart of Wasdale.

As you venture across into Wasdale, you enter through a side valley, Mosedale, cowering beneath the massive form of Pillar and ringed by fine, walking fells. When you descend to the main valley, before you opens up a view of what Nature can achieve with Borrowdale volcanic rocks, a restless, living mosaic of dark crags, lofty summits, screes, ravines, ruckles, streams and white-gash waterfalls, bound together by a turmoil of glacial debris and pinned by the arthritic fingers of gnarled old trees. Here are Coleridge's 'Monsters of the Country, bare bleak Heads, evermore doing Deeds of Darkness, weather-

plots, & storm-conspiracies in the clouds'.

Here is a place of extremes, from the highest of the Lakeland fells to the deepest of its lakes, from a landscape as pastoral and moving as any, to the savage dark tumble of ashen screes that leave you in no doubt that the waterline is but the most insignificant of thresholds. And it is this range of contrasts, heightened by the fickleness of the weather, that provides a constantly changing scene, one moment dark and glowering, the next pierced by a persistent ray of sunlight that provides a spark of light to flame the landscape into the striking brilliance that only the fields and fells of Wasdale seem to achieve.

It is a scene much photographed for calendars and book covers, and, thankfully, one of which it is impossible to tire, but, as with Ennerdale, there is much to be said for distancing yourself from the familiar images and to go in search of less conventional viewpoints from which to capture the scene. Once those sacred nooks have been discovered, wait among them until the end of the day, when, as the sun goes down and for long after, the fellsides reflect the glow of the sky, bouncing deep red, purple and bronze into the shifting shadows of scree and forest.

AROUND ENNERDALE

In spite of a long-standing reputation as a depressing place, 'claustrophobically blanketed' in dark pines, the long valley of Ennerdale is at last beginning to see the light. The cloak of trees, for so long the object of criticism, is gradually being thinned and cleared. Walks are being introduced through and around the valley that appeal to walkers of all standards, and still in the early stages of its eastbound journey, the Northern Coast-to-Coast Walk, renowned for its quality, passes down the length of Ennerdale before crossing to Honister Pass and Borrowdale.

At the head of the dale, Pillar dominates, with Steeple close by, always peering across the expanse of the lake or as mountain cameos through gaps in the trees. But best of all there is no unauthorised vehicular access beyond Bowness Knott, the dale is the preserve of pedestrians only, and all the better for it.

This walk is in two parts that may be dealt with separately if preferred. As a complete walk it is long, though never physically arduous, and is best reserved for a long summer's day. The first part circles Ennerdale Water; the second visits the forests at the head of the valley, returning easily along a woodland track.

From the woodland car park, go left to cross the River Ehen and continue a short way ahead, around water treatment works, then follow a broad track down to the lake shore **(1)**. Arrival at the edge of this substantial lake, across which the swelling sides of Great Borne and Starling Dodd soar bulkily upwards, is an inspiring moment.

A good path skirts the lake's shore, never far from the water until it encounters the rocky thrust of Anglers' Crag. Strong walkers can leave the path a little before Anglers' Crag and clamber over its summit for a splendid view of the valley. A less demanding option continues at a lower level, through the fractured base of the crag. Close by, a small headland jutting into the lake is known as Robin Hood's Chair, though there is scant evidence that this legendary hero ever ventured this far.

Once beyond Anglers' Crag the path continues pleasantly to the head of the lake **(2)**, where a path sweeps round to join the main valley trail at Irish Bridge. By this route you can shorten the day and return along the northern shore of the lake.

When the path starts heading for Irish Bridge, however, keep ahead to meet a forest

Pillar and the Ling Mell Plantation (Ennerdale)

FACT FILE

Start/Finish Woodland car park, GR 085154
Distance 8.5km (11½ miles)
Height gain 75m (245ft)
Walking time 4-5 hours
Type of walk Long, but easy-going on good paths and forest trails. The Liza Path option, if taken, can be tiring where tree-felling has taken place

The Route in Brief

Start Leave the woodland car park and cross the River Ehen, following track down to lake shore.
1 Follow path along southern shore, past Anglers' Crag, and continue to head of lake.
2 Keep ahead into plantation, and follow woodland trail or Liza Path to bridge across River Liza.
3 Return on main valley trail to Bowness Knott and take path down to northern lake shore.
4 Follow shoreline round to cross River Ehen. Go R and re-cross river to return to start.

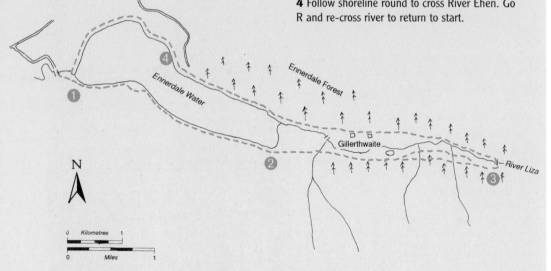

trail that runs on across Woundell Beck, by a concrete causeway, and above the River Liza into Ling Mell Plantation. A number of walks have been constructed through the Ennerdale plantations and the Liza Path is one of them, developed in 1985.

You now have a choice of routes. Either follow the main forest trail, by far the easiest option, or pursue the Liza Path as it leaves the trail for a narrow trod through trees at the forest edge. It re-emerges to pass Moss Dub, a small, overgrown tarn, before diving back into cover roughly parallel to the river. Along the way you pass an area of ancient settlements, probably Bronze Age, before the path reaches Low Beck. Here it returns to the main forest trail to cross the beck, though it can usually be crossed on the direct line, other than when in spate. From time to time forest clearance work makes progress along the Liza Path difficult. High Beck also needs to be crossed, by a footbridge, and in due course the Path rises to meet the forest trail for the last time near a bridge over the River Liza **(3)**.

Across the river, the main valley trail is soon reached. It goes right, through continuing forest to reach the splendidly set Black Sail Youth Hostel, but our way lies left, following the broad trail all the way to Bowness Knott car park. Close by the car park, a path leaves the main trail to go down to the lake shore **(4)**, which is now followed closely around the northern loop of the lake to reach a bridge over the River Ehen, from where the starting point is but a short distance to the right, back across the Ehen.

STEEPLE TO CAW FELL AND IRON CRAG

This trip along the south Ennerdale skyline is a demanding but appealing walk with excellent views once the main ridge across Scoat Fell and Haycock is reached. Virtually all the hard work goes into reaching the top of Steeple, one of Lakeland's most attractive peaks, though some reserves of energy will be needed for a descent that spars for a while with deep heather and boulders.

With no unauthorised motor access to Ennerdale, the walk must begin at the Bowness Knott car park, though shrewd walkers might consider staying overnight at the youth hostel, starting the walk from there, saving about 6km (3³/₄ miles).

From Bowness Knott take the broad trail heading into Ennerdale until, past the end of the lake, you can cross the River Liza by a concrete bridge. Beyond, the track leads across fields into the end of Ling Mell Plantation **(1)**, where it bears left. Follow it,

until you can ascend diagonally right on another track through the trees, with fairly easy progress taking you up on to the open fell of Lingmell.

The continuing path rises to a summit cairn perched on a boulder, following which you descend slightly to cross Low Beck, then setting about the broad base of the north ridge of Steeple. As you climb, so the ridge narrows and steepens, rising rockily to a fine, airy summit **(2)** with good views of Pillar to the north-east, and across Mirklin Cove to Haycock and the onward route.

A brief stony descent followed by a short, sharp pull takes you on to the edge of Little Scoat Fell, the easterly and higher (but physically smaller) half of Scoat Fell, with Great Scoat Fell lying along the wall to the southwest. As you ascend from Steeple you will need to divert left a little to reach the top of Little Scoat Fell.

The substantial wall across the top of Scoat Fell is, paradoxically, known as the Ennerdale

Steeple

Fence, an upland intake wall intended to discourage sheep from journeying out of bounds. Wall or 'fence', it now serves admirably to guide you south-west down a grassy dip and up to Haycock **(3)** before continuing by a brief rocky stairway beside Little Gowder Crag and on to the sprawling, shapeless, grassy expanse of Caw Fell.

The wall now leads you on unerringly to Iron Crag **(4)**, also known as Ennerdale Fell, the easy ascent leading to a gate through the wall by means of which the summit cairn may be reached.

A direct descent now for the plantation below Silver Cove is likely only to encounter deep heather and boulders, with the cliffs of Iron Crag also to contend with. Rather easier is a retreat to the col with Caw Fell from where a second wall leads down to and courts Silvercove Beck. When the wall starts bending to the left, leave it and contour on to the broad ridge descending northwards from near the summit of Caw Fell, where you will find a path that will hasten you down to the forest below along the line of Woundell Beck. By following this down you will return to familiar ground at the base of Ling Mell Plantation, from where you can retrace your steps to Bowness Knott.

Ennerdale Water with Pilllar, Scoat Fell and Steeple beyond

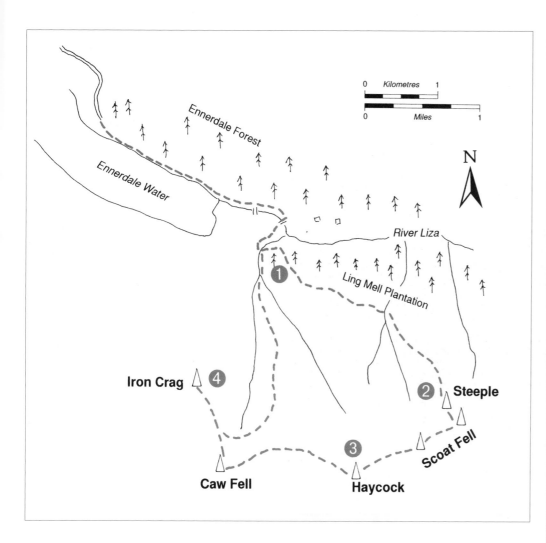

0   Kilometres   1

0   Miles   1

N

Ennerdale Forest

Ennerdale Water

River Liza

Ling Mell Plantation

1

Iron Crag △ **4**

2 △ **Steeple**

△

3 △ *Scoat Fell*

△

Caw Fell   △ **Haycock**

FACT FILE

Start/Finish Bowness Knott car park,
GR 109153
Distance 20km (12½miles)
Height gain 915m (3000ft)
Walking time 6 hours
Type of walk A long and demanding walk far
from outside help. Although the highest part of the
walk is straightforward, the final section involves
crossing some rough ground to reach a path

The Route in Brief

Start Walk from the car park to the concrete
bridge over the River Liza and cross the field
beyond to enter Ling Mell Plantation.

1 Cross the top of Lingmell and descend a little to
cross Low Beck before ascending the narrowing
north ridge of Steeple.

2 Continue by a short steep climb to Scoat Fell,
before following summital ridge wall over to
Haycock.

3 Follow wall down through Little Gowder Crag
and on to grassy Caw Fell, pressing on to take in
Iron Crag.

4 Return from Iron Crag summit to col below Caw
Fell and follow second wall down into Silver Cove,
later contouring across to path on northwards
descending ridge, before re-entering woodland
near Woundell Beck. Retrace outward steps to
Bowness Knott.

GREENDALE AND SEATALLAN

Above: Middle Fell from near Greendale Tarn

Opposite: Buckbarrow guards the entrance to Greendale Tarn

The craggy flanks of Buckbarrow and Middle Fell are much in evidence from the back roads around Nether Wasdale, but behind their bold front the grassy spread of Nether Wasdale Common, rising to its highest point on Seatallan, and the beautifully sited Greendale Tarn, are out of sight and seldom visited. It is the apparent shapelessness of Seatallan that perhaps deters many walkers, but this tour of Greendale, Seatallan and the adjoining minor top, Middle Fell, will be found to be one of many delights, and quite a few surprises.

From the grass and bracken beside the road at Greendale, a clear path sets off towards an obvious gully down which Greendale Gill displays a number of attractive cascades. A little steepness starts the day, but this relents a touch as a corner is rounded where you gain a better view of the gill. From the corner, a narrow path may be seen soaring upwards on to Middle Fell and it is by this way that the walk concludes.

Meanwhile, continue along the path above the true left bank of the gill, with both the path

Start/Finish Off-road parking at Greendale, GR 145056
Distance 8km (5 miles)
Height gain 735m (2410ft)
Walking time 3-4 hours
Type of walk A steep start through a rocky ravine gives on to grassy slopes. There are two steepish climbs, on to Seatallan and Middle Fell, from which a rocky descent leads back to the valley

The Route in Brief

Start Leave Greendale and ascend into the ravine of Greendale Gill, continuing to Greendale Tarn.
1 Cross the outflow (or go round the tarn) and ascend the steep grassy slopes to Seatallan.
2 Drop south of east to broad boggy col with Middle Fell, and follow cairned path to summit.
3 Continue with path, descending back to the start.

and gill meeting at a narrowing of the ravine, a perfect place for a breather. Quite a few streams feed into the gill at this point, hence the name Tongues Gills.

Continue with the line of Greendale Gill and as the gradient collapses completely so the cliffs of Middle Fell come into view, opposing the gentler grassy flank of Seatallan. At any time you can cross the gill and set off up the slopes of Seatallan but there is greater merit in continuing to Greendale Tarn **(1)**, concealed

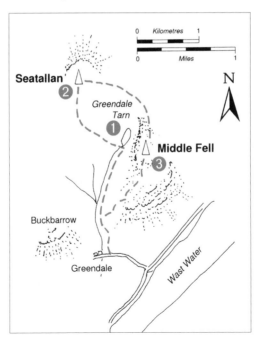

until the last moment by a small morainic plug. Though much less than an hour's walk from civilisation, beside this peaceful tarn you could be in another world. It takes a determined effort to raise yourself to cross the gill (or walk round to the northern end of the tarn) and tackle the slopes of Seatallan. There is no path to follow, simply an instinct for the easiest line, and this will lead you on to the vast summit plateau, at the northern end of which a trig **(2)** overlooking Blengdale marks the highest point. The large mound of stones on the summit are thought to be an ancient tumulus.

From Seatallan, if you descend south of east you will come to a broad boggy col with adjoining Middle Fell, across which a path materialises and rises through a much rockier landscape, dotted with small bright-eyed tarns, to the top of Middle Fell **(3)**. The path is cairned from above the col, though it is never in doubt, and provides excellent views of the hinterland of the ancient Copeland Forest – Haycock, Scoat Fell and Red Pike, against which Scoat Tarn and Low Tarn rest darkly.

The path continues over the top of Middle Fell and descends through numerous rock outcrops, easily avoiding difficulties. Lower down, good views appear of the screes spilling into Wast Water from Illgill Head, against which the bright greens of the valley pastures make a vibrant contrast. Gradually the descending path brings you back to the path corner noticed on the ascent, from where your outward steps are easily retraced.

BLACK SAIL PASS AND PILLAR BY THE HIGH LEVEL ROUTE

Far from being the slender obelisk one might expect, Pillar is a rough and rugged mountain of inspiring proportions. To Mosedale, branching from the head of Wasdale, Pillar presents a steep but fairly innocuous aspect, quite the opposite from the face overlooking Ennerdale. For here the glaciers of creation have been hard at work, sculpting the northern face of Pillar into a striking display of rock scenery that will stir the heart of any fell wanderer.

As if that is not enough, on the Ennerdale face stands Pillar Rock, an audacious structure that had it formed the true summit of the mountain would indeed have justified the name. The ascent of Pillar Rock is not for walkers: it requires rock climbing skills.

This walk, which ascends the good track through Mosedale to Black Sail Pass, leaves the main line of ascent for Pillar, to visit the environs of Pillar Rock and climbs steeply on to Pillar itself.

Overleaf: Pillar Rock

Take the path behind the Wasdale Head Inn along the banks of Mosedale Beck. Go left through a gate marked Black Sail Pass. Once past Ritson's Force the path drops a little to the floor of Mosedale. Steadily, it presses on into Mosedale and starts to climb, half right, to cross Gatherstone Beck. A little effort is needed to round the bulging shoulder across the beck, but the gradient soon eases and the path trundles gently along to a final short pull to the top of Black Sail Pass (1).

From the top of the pass, go left along a path that skirts below Looking Stead, a modest fell top but well worth visiting for it displays the onward route outstandingly.

The High Level Route leaves the main line on to Pillar just beyond Looking Stead, at a small cairn. Discovered by John Wilson Robinson, a pioneer fell walker and rock climber, the High Level Route traverses below the crags of Green Cove and Hind Cove to reach the cairn named in his honour.

At this isolated cairn, the full splendour of Pillar Rock bursts into view, throwing down an almost arrogant challenge to everyone, and sure to make any fell walker wish for once they were also competent crag hoppers. Pillar Rock spires from a broad base of rock and scree, splitting into three distinct sections as it rises. On the right is Low Man, soaring to the knuckled top of High Man, the highest point of Pillar Rock, separated from the third section, Pisgah, by the Jordan Gap. To increase the drama, the foreground is uniquely compromised by another massive crag, the Shamrock, half obscuring the fortress of Pillar Rock and lending remarkable perspective to the whole configuration.

Beyond Robinson's Cairn (2) the path dips to an easy low rock ridge, and on to the start of the Shamrock Traverse, an exciting, well-defined, but rather exposed route to the top of Pillar (3). At one point you arrive tantalisingly close to Pisgah, but you must turn your back on it to tackle the steep, loose, but otherwise easy path to the summit of Pillar, which, compared with what has gone before, comes as a bare and bald surprise. The highest point is marked by a trig point and a shelter cairn.

Retreat down the eastern ridge of Pillar back to the top of Black Sail Pass and retrace your steps from there.

Start/Finish Car park at Wasdale Head,
GR 187088
Distance 12km (7½ miles)
Height gain 820m (2690ft)
Walking time 5 hours
Type of walk Strenuous, rugged and occasionally exposed route in places on loose scree, though overall straightforward

The Route in Brief

Start Leave Wasdale Head, following signposted path to Black Sail Pass.
1 Go L from pass to Looking Stead, and just beyond branch R on to High Level Route. Continue to Robinson's Cairn.
2 Follow rough and loose track of Shamrock Traverse, and ascend loose scree path to top of Pillar mountain.
3 Retreat down E ridge to Black Sail Pass, and retrace outward route from there.

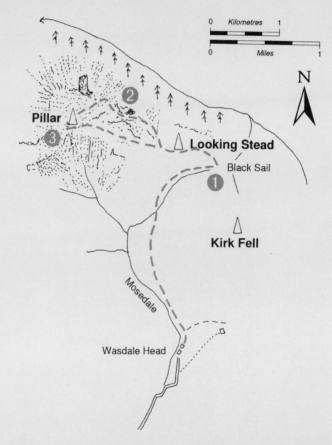

101

THE MOSEDALE HORSESHOE

This extended embrace of Mosedale, near the head of Wasdale, follows the valley's watershed throughout and so imposes a strenuous but fulfilling round on walkers. The start and finish may be modified to produce a shorter variant, by omitting both Kirk Fell and Yewbarrow, but it is better to leave this walk until time, conditions and personal fitness combine to produce what will be one of the most memorable day's fell wandering. No apology is made for including Steeple: the walk is already tough, so a little more will pass unnoticed!

From Wasdale Head Inn you set off for Black Sail Pass, but only until the intake wall is reached, at a gate. With the open valley ahead and the soaring fellside of Kirk Fell above, simply indulge in geometrical precision by ascending in a straight line, north-east, up the slopes of Kirk Fell. Wainwright's 'turf-clutching crawl' has not improved with age and it will be with weary legs that the top of Kirk Fell (1) is reached. As you cross a couple of natural dykes at the top of the ascent, so the south-west summit comes into view, close by an old fenceline.

Follow the descending fence north-west through the rocks and scree of Kirkfell Crags, awkward and loose in places, until you reach the top of Black Sail Pass (2). Those who have no stomach for the assault on Kirk Fell and who walked to this point through Mosedale, may well be waiting for you here.

Cross Black Sail Pass and set off north-west on to Looking Stead, a minor summit with a grandstand view over the northern face of Pillar and the dark conifer-cloaked flanks of Ennerdale. The ongoing path to Pillar rises in a series of grassy and rocky steps, a fine line with striking views. The top of Pillar (3) is rather bald, the highest point identified by a trig point and shelter cairn. From near the northern edge of the summit plateau there is a sensational view down to Pillar Rock.

An easy descent leads across Wind Gap to climb the bouldery unnamed summit at the top of Black Crag. Press on above Mirk Cove and follow a wall to the top of Scoat Fell. This elongated fell is divided into Little Scoat Fell (4), reached first and higher, and Great Scoat Fell. Between the two a spur branches off to

Left: Pillar from the summit of Hay Stacks
Right: Yewbarrow, the end of the Mosedale Horseshoe

FACT FILE

Start/Finish Wasdale Head car park, GR 187088
Distance 15km (9½ miles) – plus Steeple
Height gain 1440m (4725ft) – plus Steeple
Walking time 6-7 hours
Type of walk Well-defined paths throughout, but an immense amount of height gain makes this a very demanding walk

The Route in Brief

Start From Wasdale Head Inn take the path for the Black Sail Pass, leaving this after the intake gate and ascending the very steep slopes of Kirk Fell in a straight line.

1 From the top of Kirk Fell follow an old fenceline NW to descend through Kirkfell Crags to Black Sail Pass. **Variant:** Omit Kirk Fell and ascend directly to Black Sail Pass.

2 Ascend NW on to Looking Stead, continuing to Pillar.

3 Continue over unnamed summit (Black Crag) and by wall on to Little Scoat Fell. **Variant:** Visit Steeple.

4 From Little Scoat Fell head SSE on to Red Pike, and continue with path to Dore Head. **Variant:** Descend back to Mosedale from Dore Head. Avoid bad erosion by keeping to the north of a scree gully – the descent is steep, slippery and rather exposed.

5 Climb up through Stirrup Crag (avoidable on the right flank) and cross Yewbarrow.

6 Descend steeply and awkwardly, with care, through Dropping Crag and Bell Rib to reach Overbeck Bridge.

7 Walk back along the road to Wasdale Head.

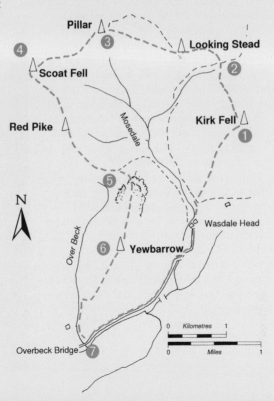

descend quickly to a col linking Steeple. Although evidently not along the watershed, Steeple is too good to miss and the modest expenditure of energy required to include it unlikely to evoke distress.

A good path leads south-east from Little Scoat Fell on to Red Pike, and from there continues to Dore Head (**5**), immediately below Stirrup Crag on the northern flank of Yewbarrow. From Dore Head you can truncate the walk by descending directly into Mosedale, keeping on grass to the left of a badly eroded spill of scree. This descent is steep and with a sense of exposure, and likely to be troublesome in winter conditions or after rain.

To complete the round, you attack the grim face of Stirrup Crag, through which an entertaining way is readily found. Walkers with no taste for such confrontation need only move right, toward Over Beck, to find a steep grassy slope offering an easier line on to Yewbarrow.

Continue across the airy top of Yewbarrow (**6**), though in late July and August a diversion to the bilberry-laden slopes overlooking Wasdale could prove tasty. As the ridge starts to drop, a good path leads you down through Dropping Crag and Bell Rib to Overbeck Bridge (**7**). This descent requires care and can be slippery in almost all conditions. A winter descent is likely to prove awkward and may need the use of crampons.

From Overbeck Bridge, the start at Wasdale Head is 3km (2 miles) along the road, a regular stroll that will prove welcome.

ILLGILL HEAD
AND THE WAST WATER SCREES

In what promises to be a lively and entertaining outing, this walk traverses the long whaleback ridge of Illgill Head and Whin Rigg from which the famed screes of Wast Water plummet. When that is done, a steep descent leads to the base of the screes, across which a path scampers with inelegant haste back to the head of Wasdale.

With the deep darkness of the lake, the deepest in Lakeland, set against towering slopes of unstable scree which continue unseen into the very depths of the lake (18m/60ft below sea level), this walk is one of remarkable contrasts, a fascinating and energetic round.

In Wasdale

From the car park near the camp site a track heads across a concrete bridge. Follow this and then turn left along the left bank of a stream. Move right, beneath Brackenclose, a climbers' hut, to find a path issuing from the far corner of its grounds. Begin ascending through Fence Wood on an old corpse road (by means of which the dead

were carried to consecrated ground) to reach the open fell. When a wall is encountered rising on to Illgill Head, follow it: it is a secure guide (almost) to the cairn that marks the summit of the fell (1). A trig point nearby is marginally lower but is a superb viewpoint.

Press on across the grassy summit ridge to reach Whin Rigg (2), passing a couple of small tarns *en route*. Whin Rigg has two summits; that to the east is the higher, while its neighbour commands the better position.

Continue in the same direction, dropping easily to a cairn about 150m/yd before the ravine of Greathall Gill. The cairn marks the start of a steeply descending path heading right, finding a way down parallel with the gill but never entering it. At the foot of the ravine follow a stone wall (3), right, to a track above the lake shore. Go past a pump house on a small headland and on to a path that traverses the screes.

Resisting the temptation to hasten, move along the path, which at first is well-defined. Gradually you encounter a spread of larger boulders that handicap progress for a while and calls for boulder-hopping agility, before the path resumes a more acceptable format and eases across the brackeny fellside to a track passing Wasdale Head Hall Farm. Beyond, the track returns you to the bridge at the start of the walk.

Illgill Head, Whin Rigg, and the Wast Water Screes

FACT FILE

Start/Finish Camp site car park, Wasdale, GR 182074
Distance 14km (8¾ miles)
Height gain 615m (2015ft)
Walking time 4-5 hours
Type of walk A long and steep start leads to an easy grassy ridge. Steep descent then precedes a potentially intimidating traverse along the base of screes

The Route in Brief
Start Leave the car park and cross a bridge, going past Brackenclose to rise into Fence Wood. A wall beyond leads steeply upwards to the top of Illgill Head.
1 Continue along ridge to Whin Rigg.
2 A short way beyond Whin Rigg, descend steeply beside Greathall Gill to reach wall.
3 Go R, past pump house, and along path above waterline. Some awkward manoeuvring in the middle precedes an improving path to Wasdale Head Hall Farm, and a return to the start.

Wasdale Head Hall Farm

Wast Water

Illgill Head
1

Wasdale Hall

3

2 Whin Rigg

N

0 Kilometres 1
0 Miles 1

6

THE SCAFELLS

To wander about the precipices and rocky corridors of the Scafells is to focus not on the whole but on the elements underfoot, the immediate rocky rise or buttress, and the imminent, sometimes weary steps ahead. And even if you step back and view the Scafells, say, from Bowfell, Esk Pike, Great Gable or the ridge of Red Pike above Mosedale, the view is often still dominated by the individual elements that stand out from the overall scene in an exaggerated way. The great gap of Mickledore always draws the eye, while above the Corridor Route, rising optimistically from Sty Head, it is impossible not to be fascinated by the savagery of Piers Gill.

Boulders and scree predominate, for there is little room for the prerequisites of survival, for trees and shrubs, and not much more tolerance of the harsh grasses and mosses that somehow manage to exist. Water, as ever, finds a place, in secret high mountain tarns and valley lakes and in the myriad streams that cascade hastily from the unwelcoming heights. Only to the south, where mountain meets moorland, does the savagery relent a little, substituting for savage, a landscape that is bleak and harsh; Eskdale Moss, inhabited since prehistoric times, is a worthy concomitant of England's highest fells. Along with the rocky summits that flow from the Scafells, Eskdale Moss provides just another form of defence, keeping from the casual eye the mysteries of the central massif.

From this windswept moorland, the core of the region rises as an excruciatingly rough series of summits from Slight Side and Scafell, across Mickledore to Scafell Pike, Broad Crag and Ill Crag, before reaching Great End, sentinel of Borrowdale. The easiest of approaches rise from Wasdale, but even entry into this glamorous glen involves long detours from the main roadways of Lakeland. For this reason, Scafell Pike is most frequently ascended from Seathwaite in Borrowdale or from Langdale. Scafell, however, often proves one step too far from either of these starting points and has at its disposal an array of deterrents against anyone who thinks they know better. Mickledore itself, leaned on by dark, vertical crags, can be an intimidating place. On either side, broken rocks slither to the valleys below, while the way through the crags above, by a passage known as Broad Stand, is completely beyond anyone lacking rock climbing skills. Coleridge found a way down it, which he described in 1802, but his survival was more good luck than good management.

If you persist, the Wasdale flank will yield Lord's Rake, a roller-coaster approach traversing the northern face of the fell, while the base of the East Buttress gives up a thin line that leads to Foxes Tarn and a steep pathway to the top. When either of these is conquered, the return awaits.

For unadulterated pleasure, what might be called the connoisseur's approach, there is nothing to beat the long walk from Brotherikeld into Eskdale and the Great Moss. So fascinating is this vast, neglected region that you may well spend more time there than scaling the heights.

Harry Griffin's 'Roof of England' will always draw the crowds, bathed in various shades of expertise, but mere success in reaching the top of the mountain tells you little about the mountain itself. For that you need more time and the patience to explore. Then and only then will you get some idea why the Scafells rank among the best in Britain.

The Scafells from the Three Tarns

THE SCAFELLS FROM WASDALE

In spite of the ascent from Wasdale being the shortest of the routes up Scafell Pike, this combination with Scafell is never going to be a simple stroll, indeed it is *very* demanding and can be intimidating for less experienced walkers at the best of times. In winter conditions, this circuit is a major undertaking, only to be contemplated by well-experienced and fully-equipped winter walkers. But as an exercise in walk planning the format of the route cannot be bettered.

The major difficulties are associated with Scafell and not Scafell Pike, leaving those with no appetite for crag-related exploration to call it a day on reaching the highest summit in England; Scafell will always await another day and does have less complex approaches.

From the car park near the camp site, head for the concrete bridge that spans Lingmell Gill and turn left, following the stream, keeping Brackenclose, a climbers'

Left: View back across Lord's Rake to Scafell Pike
Opposite: The summit of Scafell

club hut, on your right. Cross a footbridge and keep along the line of the gill. Beyond a fence, ignore a path going left on to the shoulder of Lingmell (though strong walkers could add this fell to the day's walk and rejoin this route at Lingmell col).

Continue climbing with the gill until, after a wall, you need to cross it once more to gain Brown Tongue **(1)**, framed by streams and directly below Hollow Stones and Mickledore. As you reach the edge of Hollow Stones you have a choice of routes. Either go left along a cairned path to Lingmell col, from where a stony path leads upwards, directly to the summit of Scafell Pike, or continue up through Hollow Stones and the towering rock scenery beyond to reach Mickledore by a steep loose-scree gully. Another rocky path, going left from Mickledore, will take you to the highest point in England. The former is the easier, the latter much more demanding physically and in terms of mountain walking ability.

From Scafell Pike **(2)** take the rocky path down to Mickledore **(3)** and cross this narrow link to the edge of Scafell Crag, and there descend right, down a badly eroded path keeping close to the base of the crag. This takes you to the foot of Lord's Rake, now a rather bare gully rising between the crags of

FACT FILE

Start/Finish
Car park adjoining camp site at Wasdale, GR 182074

Distance 10km (6¼ miles)
Height gain 1040m (3410ft)
Walking time 5-6 hours
Type of walk A strenuous day, with difficult going on Lord's Rake

The Route in Brief

Start Leave the car park, cross Lingmell Gill and follow the stream, left, over a wooden footbridge and on to cross a wall below Brown Tongue.
1 Continue ahead, ascending to Hollow Stones, and there either go L to Lingmell col by a cairned route, ascending, R, to Scafell Pike from there, or keep climbing up a loose scree gully to Mickledore and turn L for Scafell Pike.
2 Follow rocky path to Mickledore.
3 Cross Mickledore and descend beneath Scafell Crag to a level path below Lord's Rake and climb the rake with care to reach the broad shoulder beyond, up which a rough path ascends to the top of Scafell.
4 Descend roughly W, down grassy slopes over Green How to reach path above Fence Wood, and turn R to pass Brackenclose and return to the start.

Scafell and a subsidiary buttress on the right. At the start of the rake, a cross carved in the rock commemorates the death in 1903 of four pioneer rock climbers who fell from the crags above this spot.

Set off up Lord's Rake and scramble awkwardly to the first obvious col, a narrow transverse ledge barely wide enough to stand on. A short descent and re-ascent takes you to a second col from which the third can be seen ahead. To reach it, another descent on an eroded path precedes more of the same as you climb out of the rake.

As you leave the rake, turn left and ascend a rocky path to a small plateau with a minor top, Symonds Knott, on your left. A branching path, heading right, soon leads you to the massively cairned summit **(4)**.

After so much rock work it will come as a surprise that the way back to Wasdale lies down sweeping grassy flanks, roughly west, over Green How to meet an old corpse road above the walls of Fence Wood. Turn right here to descend to Brackenclose, where your outward route is rejoined.

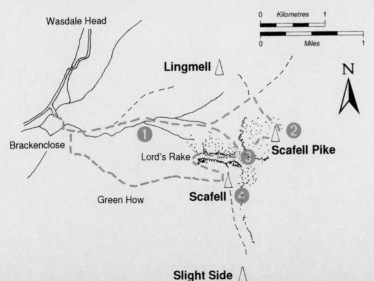

LINGMELL AND SCAFELL PIKE BY THE CORRIDOR ROUTE

The Corridor Route runs from Sty Head to Lingmell Col and is one of the finest approaches to Scafell Pike and the often neglected, Lingmell. There is a little mild scrambling at its start and a short passage that is slightly exposed as you pass the spectacular ravine of Piers Gill.

The walk returns by the outward route but the finish can be varied by descending steeply to the Corridor Route from Broad Crag Col (between Scafell Pike and Broad Crag), or by reversing Walk 32 and climbing across the rocky terrain of Broad Crag, Ill Crag and even Great End, before surrendering the heights and plunging valleywards in the company of Grains Gill. This combined version is undoubtedly one of the finest routes in the Lake District, but it is long and tiring and should be reserved for a fine summer's day.

From Seathwaite keep ahead through the farm buildings to follow a broad track running south to Stockley Bridge (1). Once over the bridge, go through a gate, ignore a path on the left and tackle the bulging shoulder directly ahead, up which the path zigzags a few times and passes through a gate in the intake wall to move right towards the stand of larches above the ravine of Taylorgill Force.

The ongoing path is never in doubt and rises rockily to a stony trail leading to a bridge spanning Styhead Gill. Beyond the bridge the path wanders easily on toward Styhead Tarn, peacefully reposed beneath the shoulder of Seathwaite Fell and set against one of the most breathtaking backdrops imaginable, formed by the great buttresses of Great End, Broad Crag, Scafell Pike and Lingmell. If you chance this way in winter, the tarn and its surrounds is a good indicator of what you might expect to find along the Corridor Route in terms of snow and ice – *do* heed any such warning, since a slip above Piers Gill could have terminal consequences.

Soon the path reaches Sty Head (2), a busy mountain pass and crossroads from where the Corridor Route (formerly called the Guides Route) is in view, but not instantly obvious. It links a series of grassy ledges, interspersed with rocky wedges, across the lower slopes of

Lingmell from the Corridor Route

Great End and Broad Crag. To reach it, look for an initially indistinct path leaving Sty Head heading to the right of a low hill below the cliffs of Great End, or follow the more prominent Esk Hause path for a short distance until

the Corridor Route appears on the right.

Soon after leaving Sty Head, the Corridor Route meets Skew Gill, a narrow gully of crumbling red rock that needs a little hands-on experience. Take the constructed path above and continue across the head of Greta Gill, pursuing a long and splendid rocky path, passing the dramatic ravine of Piers Gill and crossing below Broad Crag Col, before arriving at Lingmell Col (3). The route is never in doubt and well-cairned.

From the col, the way up to Scafell Pike is also well-cairned, but it is worth diverting first along a grassy trod to visit Lingmell itself; it is an outstanding vantage point, offers a good view of the rocky trail up to Scafell Pike and is quite often neglected. Lingmell is easily reached across a wall and up grassy slopes to a fine upstanding cairn and a magnificent view of Great Gable.

Return directly to the col and start up the long stony trail that treks to the top of Scafell Pike (4), where arrival is a satisfying, if invariably un-private, moment.

The possibility of returning by other routes has already been mentioned; to return by the outward route, however, is considerably easier and quicker. You could, of course, visit Lingmell on the way back rather than on the ascent.

Left: The upper section of Piers Gill: Great Gable and Kirk Fell beyond

FACT FILE

Start/Finish Seathwaite Farm, GR 236123. Limited off-road parking. Do not block gates
Distance 13km (8 miles)
Height gain 850m (2790ft)
Walking time 5 hours
Type of walk A long and rocky walk with some mild scrambling and occasional exposure. Can be problematical in poor visibility, especially at Lingmell Col. Do **not** attempt to pass above Piers Gill if the path is iced over, unless you are wearing crampons and equipped with an ice axe

The Route in Brief
Start From Seathwaite set off southwards to Stockley Bridge.
1 Cross the bridge, through a gate and climb a shoulder ahead to another gate in the intake wall. Follow the ensuing path upwards and along the line of Styhead Gill to Sty Head.

2 Locate the Corridor Route below Great End, and follow this rocky thoroughfare to Lingmell Col.
3 Ascend from the col to Lingmell, return and climb up on to Scafell Pike.
4 Return by the same route.

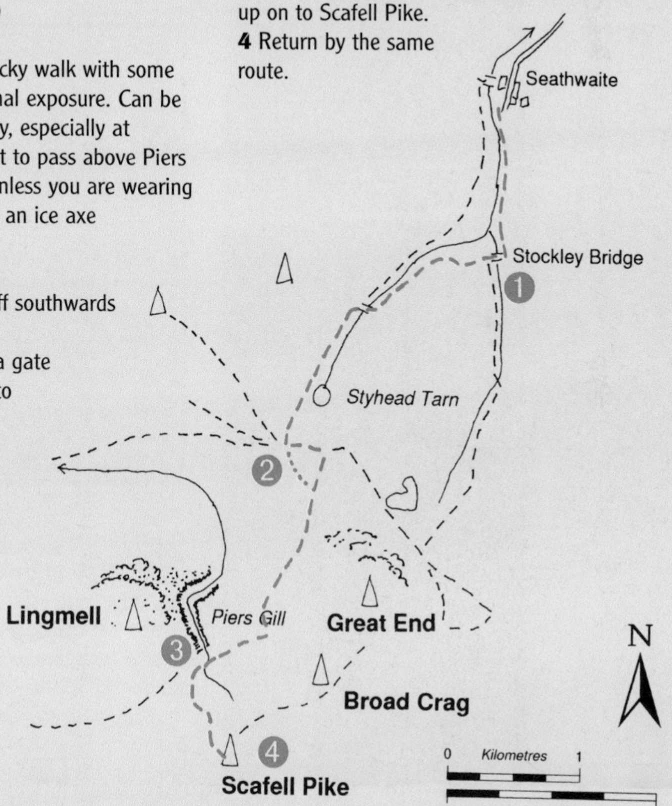

Seathwaite

Stockley Bridge

Styhead Tarn

Lingmell

Piers Gill

Great End

Broad Crag

Scafell Pike

N

0   Kilometres   1

0   Miles   1

ILL CRAG, BROAD CRAG AND SCAFELL PIKE FROM BORROWDALE

This long approach to Scafell Pike by way of Esk Hause provides an alternative to the ascent via Sty Head and the Corridor Route. The early stages of the walk, beyond Stockley Bridge, are enclosed by the steep sides of Seathwaite Fell, Glaramara and Allen Crags, but once Esk Hause is reached a new and splendid panorama unfolds and improves as height is gained.

The opportunity to include seldom-visited Ill Crag and its neighbour, Broad Crag, should not be missed. Both are excellent viewpoints and quiet, off-the-track oases of calm that call for little extra effort.

Leave the farm at Seathwaite heading south to Stockley Bridge **(1)**, a fine packhorse bridge demolished by floods in 1966. Over the bridge, through a gate, go left to follow a wall and path rising between the steep flanks of Seathwaite Fell and Glaramara.

This way up to Esk Hause, which becomes

Stockley Bridge

increasingly dominated by the bulk of Great End, rises gradually, following first Grains Gill (on your left) and later Ruddy Gill, which is crossed by a neatly positioned footbridge. Near the top of Ruddy Gill **(2)**, the path descends to cross the stream in a narrow ravine. On emerging, the immense, gully-riven face of Great End can be examined from the path beyond the gill. This face of Great End provides some outstanding winter climbing for experienced mountaineers.

The track beyond Ruddy Gill links Sty Head and Esk Hause, a route of prehistoric significance. Set off, left, along it, towards Esk Hause, but soon abandon it for a diverging track on the right, that leads more directly into Calf Cove **(3)**. Here you will find the last running water on this ascent. From this raised position above Esk Hause you can look back to the hause, to nearby Allen Crags and Esk Pike and the far summits of Langdale and the eastern fells. Ill Crag has a good profile from here and is sometimes mistaken for Scafell Pike.

As you climb out of Calf Cove you realise the mistake, of course, rising to gain a long

connecting ridge between Great End and Ill Crag. A section bedevilled with large boulders requires some agile foot work for a brief while, before the path settles down, bearing slightly to the right of Ill Crag. You need to leave the path to visit Ill Crag, but this minor detour across stony, but easy ground is well worthwhile and gives a fine view of Scafell Pike.

Returning to the path, descend to a rocky col, with bulky Broad Crag (4) directly above. Another detour is necessary to embrace Broad Crag's extremely bouldery summit. The way

Scafell Pike and Broad Crag col from Ill Crag

across Broad Crag is cairned, but still remains vague and very bouldery. Follow the path to the narrow, steep-sided col with Scafell Pike.

The final section, steeply upwards to Scafell

117

Start/Finish Seathwaite Farm, GR 236123. Limited off-road parking. Please do not obstruct gateways

Distance 13km (8 miles)

Height gain 920m (3020ft)

Walking time 5 hours

Type of walk A rough mountain walk, largely on rocky trails and bouldery terrain, but otherwise straightforward in good conditions. Some risk of confusion in poor visibility and/or in winter conditions, when sections can be icy and awkward

The Route in Brief

Start Leave Seathwaite and go S down the valley to Stockley Bridge.

1 Cross the bridge to a gate and go L on a path by a wall. Ascend with the path to reach the top of Ruddy Gill.

2 Beyond Ruddy Gill go left for a short distance, then R on a rising track to Calf Cove.

3 Climb out of Calf Cove, and pursue a bouldery trail first to Ill Crag and then Broad Crag.

4 Descend to narrow col with Scafell Pike, and climb upwards (awkward in winter conditions) through rocks to the summit shoulder, and then by a cairned path to the summit. To return, either retrace your outward journey or select one of the variations described.

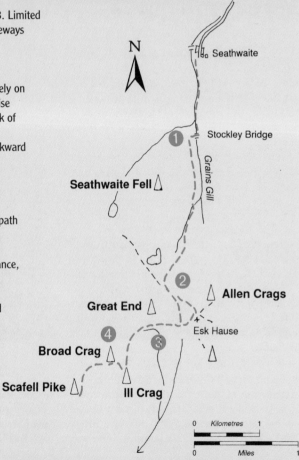

Pike, is without difficulty in summer conditions, but can be awkward under snow and ice. At these times, certainly, an ice axe is needed and probably crampons, too. If there is any mist around the summit, take care to note the way back to the col, an easy undertaking in good visibility but made difficult in poor conditions by a proliferation of cairns.

Wordsworth's 'stillness... not of this world' to which he and his companions 'paused, and kept silence to listen' is a rare commodity these days. Only once in all my years of fell wandering have I experienced solitude on Scafell Pike's summit – it was past midnight on a July summer's day in 1978, when gale force winds and rain lashed the landscape!

About this craggy summit, of course, there are many niches in which to secrete oneself, away from the buzz of the highest point, overlooking Eskdale, Wasdale or Great Gable, while in the direction of Scafell, Broadcrag Tarn, tucked away to the east of Mickledore, is a splendid place to take a break and inspect the great buttresses of the adjoining fell.

With the possibility of linking this ascent to Scafell, or of returning by way of the Corridor Route, it is for you to decide. Merely to retrace your outward steps is no disappointment: the return journey holds equal fascination and can be varied by descending from the top of Ruddy Gill directly to Sty Head, or by extending the walk to include Great End, an easy addition if taken in descent.

SEATHWAITE FELL, SPRINKLING TARN AND GREAT END

In the gather of mountains at the southernmost point of Borrowdale, the shapely wedge of Seathwaite Fell is rarely visited, yet it provides a superlative view of Great Gable and hosts an amazing assortment of tiny tarns that will greatly appeal to anyone with waterside inclinations. The largest of the tarns, Sprinkling Tarn, is briefly touched upon by the path linking Sty Head and Esk Hause, but neither this nor the maze of Seathwaite Fell's knolls and concealed tarn-filled hollows beyond spurs many walkers into a closer acquaintance.

For a short day, in any season, this brief encounter will prove to be a revelation.

Leave Seathwaite for Sty Head either by going south on the trail to Stockley Bridge and climbing west from there to pursue Styhead Gill, or by heading through the arch in the farm buildings at Seathwaite to cross the River Derwent and then heading left, below Base Brown to reach Sty Head by way of Taylorgill Force.

The former route passes below a steepish gully through Aaron Crags on Seathwaite Fell that filled with winter snows produces an interesting and straightforward direct route to the summit; without the snow, it is fairly mundane.

Many tracks radiate from Sty Head (1). One, setting off eastwards, rises conspicuously below the dark cliffs and gullies of Great End and reaches the westernmost tip of Sprinkling Tarn. A narrow path leads, left, around the tarn, through a landscape of rock outcrops and little hollows that are fascinating to explore on a clear day. The highest point of Seathwaite Fell (2)(GR 227097) is marked by a cairn and has a good view of the much higher surrounding fells. At the northern end of this mountain-bound promontory, another cairn overlooking Styhead Gill is an excellent vantage point for the Gables.

Back on the Esk Hause track, continue rising in a south-easterly direction, directly

Early morning mist over Great End and Styhead Tarn

beneath the towering ramparts of Great End, a formidable sight cloaked in winter ice. The path passes the top of Ruddy Gill, your eventual way down, and a short way on, a rising path on the right leads directly to Calf Cove. Ignore both and press on along the main path to reach a cross-shelter near the highest point of Esk Hause, below both Allen Crags and Esk Pike. The construction of the shelter is such that you should be able to combat winds from any direction.

The path on to Esk Hause (3) continues clearly and swings round in a westerly direction to enter Calf Cove, passing at a large cairn the top of the direct route from the path below.

The main path out of Calf Cove brings you on to a broad col linking the upland plateau that extends to Ill Crag and Great End (4). From the col turn right for an easy walk, over rough and rocky terrain, to the two cairns that adorn the summit of the fell. The cairn nearest to Calf Cove is the higher.

Misty conditions are not conducive to an exploration of Great End, but on a clear day the views down the gullies at the northern end of the summit are quite outstanding. Having explored, return to Calf Cove and descend to the large cairn passed on the way up from Esk Hause. Here turn left to descend the direct route, which brings you close to the top of Ruddy Gill.

Cross Ruddy Gill, then take an on-going path that drops quickly into the valley beyond. Keep heading down to cross the gill by a bridge, where it becomes Grains Gill. Beyond, the path leads on easily to a gate giving access to Stockley Bridge, from where a simple return is effected to Seathwaite.

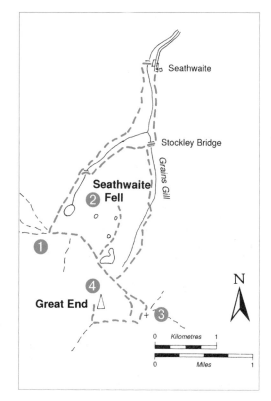

Far left: Great Gable from Sprinkling Tarn
Left: Seathwaite Fell

FACT FILE

Start/Finish Seathwaite Farm, GR 236123. Limited off-road parking. Do not obstruct gateways, please
Distance 12.5km (7¾ miles)
Height gain 810m (2655ft)
Walking time 4-5 hours
Type of walk Straightforward, on clear paths, except on Seathwaite Fell. Mostly rocky underfoot. Not advised in poor visibility

The Route in Brief

Start From Seathwaite follow either of two routes to Sty Head.
1 Take path ascending towards Esk Hause and on reaching the edge of Sprinkling Tarn, explore the hummocky terrain of Seathwaite Fell.
2 Return to the main path and ascend to Esk Hause.
3 Follow main path around Esk Hause into Calf Cove and ascend from there to Great End.
4 On the descent, either retrace steps, or cut directly to top of Ruddy Gill and descend across Ruddy Gill and down to Grains Gill and Stockley Bridge.

ESKDALE MOOR AND BURNMOOR TARN

For a walk on the wild side there is little to better this exploration of the moors south of the main Scafell massif, a place, especially when approached from Eskdale, that is indefinably attractive, and, according to legend, haunted by the spirit of a horse that bolted whilst conveying a corpse from Wasdale to Eskdale, and was never recovered.

It is, too, a region once inhabited by Bronze Age man, as stone circles on Boat How and elsewhere testify, and one to savour in summer when the surrounding fells, Illgill Head and the mighty Scafells, are thronged with walkers, and the moors are, by comparison, neglected.

The walk begins from the once industrially busy village of Boot, where the museum was formerly a corn mill and the ever-popular Eskdale to Ravenglass Railway founded on a narrow gauge railway that served an iron mine.

Left: Eskdale Fell
Right: Eel Tarn

Go over the stone arched bridge and past the mill, following a bridleway towards Brat's Moss. The route zigzags to start flanked by walls made of Eskdale granite, and, as you reach the open moor, so you find a group of stone buildings that probably served as peat houses, in which peat from the moor was dried and stored.

As you reach the last building, bear right on to Brat's Moss **(1)** and seek out a grassy mound near Brat's Hill that proves to conceal a stone circle, composed now of collapsed and standing stones and within which five burial chambers were discovered.

Ahead the path goes on to Low Longrigg, where there are more circles, and then along the easy shoulder to Boat How **(2)**, a small rocky summit.

An easy descent now leads towards Burnmoor Tarn and Burnmoor Lodge, the latter indicating that the tarn, one of the largest in Lakeland, was once used by anglers, while a line of shooting butts confirms that the moors yielded grouse for sportsmen to shoot at.

Burnmoor Tarn lies in a wide hollow, crossed by an old corpse road, and, in spite of surrounding bogginess, is an evocative place to be, where the flight of moorland birds gives shape to the wind.

FACT FILE

Start/Finish Boot, GR 176011. Very limited parking. You can ask permission at the Burnmoor Inn to park there, but do so before setting off
Distance 11km (7 miles)
Height gain 550m (1805ft)
Walking time 3-4 hours
Type of walk Some stretches are boggy, some pathless, and the ascent of Oliver Gill, steep. But on a clear day, the walk is overall straightforward

The Route in Brief

Start Leave Boot over the arched bridge, then along an enclosed track to reach the open moor. Pass derelict peat houses before heading for Brat's Moss.
1 Walk easily on to Low Longrigg and up to Boat How.
2 Descend to Burnmoor Tarn and cross footbridge before crossing Hardrigg Gill.
3 Climb through Oliver Gill and on to Great How (Eskdale Fell).
4 Descend over Whinscales towards Stony Tarn, and traverse through heather and rock outcrops towards Eel Tarn.
5 Pass N of Eel Tarn to find good track leading down to enclosing walls and a bridleway back to Boot.

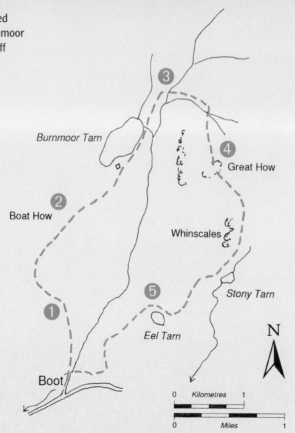

The ongoing path crosses Whillan Beck by a simple bridge, following which bear right, across a boggy stretch to cross a stream above the confluence of Hardrigg Gill (**3**) and Oliver Gill. If now you ascend the fellside above, you will find a path leading up into Oliver Gill, which narrows to an interesting ravine just north of Bleaberry How. Follow the south, true left, bank across the steep sides of the ravine before escaping on to the northern edge of Eskdale Fell. Go south, past a group of small tarns, the largest of which has a small island resplendent in summer with the bright yellow eyes of bog asphodel. Continue to the rocky topknot, Great How.

To the west you will find a way through the rocks of Great How (**4**) to a shoulder running southwards to Whinscales. The shoulder continues towards Stony Tarn, before it heads right with intermittent paths that probe rock and heather to reach Eel Tarn (**5**). None of the going over Great How is well-endowed with clear paths, making a day of good visibility essential.

A path passes north of Eel Tarn, from where you can descend on a trail, leading into the embrace of stone walls that guide you down from the moor. Through a gate a bridleway leads you back to Boot, easing down amid heavily scented gorse bushes to emerge in the main street by the arched bridge.

SCAFELL AND SLIGHT SIDE FROM ESKDALE

Protected from casual inspection from the direction of Scafell Pike by a formidable display of cliffs, Scafell, the second highest summit in England, must prove a frustrating, and for some a nerve-racking, conquest from that direction. Thankfully, there is a simpler approach through Eskdale, that cleverly picks a way round all the major obstacles, though it should not be regarded as easy.

The long walk in from Brotherikeld leads to the Great Moss, where the River Esk must be crossed, before starting upon the strenuous pull to the summit. The opportunity is taken to return over Slight Side, one of the most elusive fells of Lakeland for those bent on fulfilling a round of all the major tops.

Overleaf: Scafell, Slight Side and the Great Moss

Begin from a car park near the cattle grid (marked on the map), east of Brotherikeld. Locate a path above the nearby plantation and follow it into fields above the farm. The path heads into Eskdale and eases through the gap between Hard Knott, on which Eskdale Needle stands out prominently, and Heron Crag. This is splendid walking, especially in spring and summer, and takes you on across Lingcove Bridge (1), still pursuing the River Esk, and bound for that vast boggy expanse known as the Great Moss. Before reaching the Moss, the path passes below Scar Lathing to emerge opposite the cliffs of Cam Spout Crag. To the north of Cam Spout Crag, How Beck creates an attractive waterfall as it descends from the mountainside to join the Esk. Just above the confluence (2) it is usually possible to cross the river dryshod, but be prepared for damper possibilities.

To the right of the How Beck waterfall, scramble up a steep path into the hanging valley above until, below Mickledore and the crags of East Buttress, you can turn up beside a stream issuing from a rocky gully on the left. This leads directly to Foxes Tarn (3), probably the smallest named tarn in the Lake District. From it a repaired track leads up to the edge of the rocky summit plateau, where a left turn will take you to the summit cairn (4).

The summit is predictably a fabulous viewpoint, embracing Scotland, Wales, Ireland and the dusky galleon of the Isle of Man sailing across the Irish Sea.

From the summit the long walk down, very roughly southwards, to Slight Side (5) seems endless, but once gained you need to tackle a short scramble through rocks to the right, south-west, to reach a path that continues the descent into Cow Cove and Cat Cove (6). When you reach the ravine that houses Catcove Beck, go left above Scale Gill and work a way down to a gate in the intake wall. Go through the lower gate and cross the field to reach the farm at Taw House.

Cross a stile and go left between wall and fence to a footbridge over the Esk, beyond which the path passes round Brotherikeld Farm and runs out to the road at the foot of the Hardknott Pass. Go left to return to your starting point.

FACT FILE

Start/Finish Car park below Hardknott Pass, GR 214011
Distance 13.5km (8¼ miles)
Height gain 900m (2950ft)
Walking time 5-5½ hours
Type of walk Long walk across remote, boggy and rocky countryside. One river crossing needed, followed by a demanding ascent

The Route in Brief

Start Follow path above plantation to traverse fields into Esk valley, to Lingcove Bridge.
1 Cross bridge and ascend to Great Moss and cross River Esk above confluence with How Beck.
2 Ascend beside waterfall into steep hanging valley, turning L below East Buttress to reach Foxes Tarn.
3 Climb path to summit plateau and turn L to reach summit cairn.
4 Descend long ridge to Slight Side.
5 Go R, down through rocks to continue descending through Cow Cove and Cat Cove.
6 At Catcove Beck, turn L down Scale Gill to gate in wall (take the lower gate), and out to Taw House and Brotherikeld, from where the road is reached.

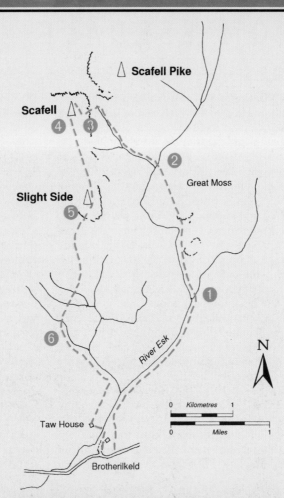

126

ACKNOWLEDGEMENTS & INDEX

I am particularly grateful to Dave Brown of DB Mountain Sports, Kendal, for the supply of boots, clothing and equipment, which kept me warm, dry and comfortable throughout the preparation of this book.

In addition, I much appreciate the generosity of Lakelovers of Bowness-on-Windermere for allowing me to use one of their excellent self-catering holiday homes.

Steve Yeates of the Ordnance Survey Press Office has very kindly supplied me with up-to-date Outdoor Leisure Maps, from which I have been able to deduce much reliable and vital information.